Memoir of a Narcissist's Daughter

Memoir
of a
Narcissist's Daughter

The story of a daughter's recovery
from the life-depleting effects
of her mother's narcissism

by Susan Lynne Arnold

ISBN: 1792006837
ISBN 13: 9781792006838

Life is a Journey

From childhood to maturity
and youth to age
From innocence to knowing
From foolishness to discretion
and then, perhaps to wisdom
From weakness to strength
or strength to weakness –
and often back again
From offense to forgiveness
From loneliness to love
From joy to gratitude
From pain to compassion
and grief to understanding
From fear to faith…
Until, looking backward or ahead
we see that victory lies ahead
not at some high place along the way
but in having made the journey
stage by stage
A sacred pilgrimage

Gates of Repentance
Rabbeinu Yonah of Gerona Spain
(1180-1263 C.E.)

Introduction

My name is Susan. I am the daughter of a highly narcissistic woman although I didn't discover this reality until I was in my forties. Then a mid-life crisis bubbled up from deep within me and I began a journey to understand and to break the life-depleting narcissist's spell which my mother had cast upon me – albeit without her having malevolent intention or any awareness of what she was doing.

Like most highly narcissistic people, my mother experienced herself as the center of the universe. Life was all about her. To feel safe she needed to control other people and situations. Intimidation and manipulation were tools she used to accomplish this control. She was incapable of empathy and therefore not able to relate compassionately with others. Instead, she required others to respond to her with adoration and blind loyalty – without questioning her ideas, motives, or actions. If these responses were not forthcoming, she reacted with distancing, passive aggressive behavior, or revenge. She presented herself to the world as an exemplary human being with an exemplary family. She was esteemed by her career peers and authored several books. Yet, underneath it all my mother probably suffered enormously from low self-esteem and a deep fear that she would be found out as unworthy. Such psychological dynamics are frequently the case with highly narcissistic people.

The child of a highly narcissistic parent tends to take one of two paths, depending upon the disposition of his/her innate personality. A sensitive and accommodating child learns to comply with the narcissistic parent's requirements for adoration, loyalty, and high performance. By complying, however, the child represses his/her feelings, develops a false identity, and engages in a codependent relationship with the parent. In adulthood s/he is likely to participate in other codependent relationships and continue to be a narcissist-enabler. In contrast to the sensitive and accommodating child, the aggressive and confrontational child of a highly narcissistic parent learns the intimidation, manipulation, and revenge techniques of the parent. As an adult s/he is likely to become highly narcissistic, requiring others to be adoring, blindly loyal, and high performing. I was a sensitive and accommodating child. I learned to repress my true feelings and become the person my mother wanted me to be. In adulthood I continued to be a narcissist-enabler. My brother, on the other hand, was an aggressive and confrontational child. He argued with our mother and learned her intimidation, manipulation, and revenge techniques. In adulthood he became highly narcissistic.

My mother died of cancer at the age of fifty. I was fourteen years old. My response to her death was to cry myself to sleep, night after night after night – alone. During the daytime, however, I courageously continued to carry a banner for my mother by overachieving, being who she had taught me to be, and always honoring her perfection and way of life. My father cried openly and often after my mother died. I thought it was my job to remain strong and not cry in his presence. My brother graduated from high school two months after our mother died and then disappeared for the entire summer, returning in time to start college in the fall.

Three years after my mother's death my fathered married Betty. Betty was an elementary school teacher who was personable, attractive, and lots of fun. When she and my father became engaged she told me she didn't want to take anyone's place; she just wanted to be my friend. Much to my surprise I quickly gravitated to Betty's kind and joyful spirit which was very different from what I had experienced with my biological mother.

I went off to college three months after my father and Betty were married. Then, before the end of my first term in college, I began to have waves of depression which caused me to frequently cry uncontrollably although I didn't know why I was crying. While I continued to do well in my studies, I was emotionally miserable. I shared my symptoms with my father and Betty who then met with our family's physician. He suggested I begin psychological counseling when the second college term ended, and he recommended a psychiatrist for me to see. I met with the psychiatrist on a monthly basis for six years. He was a profoundly helpful counselor.

It is important to note that I met with the psychiatrist at a time in history before the term "Narcissistic Personality Disorder" (NPD) had been created and defined. And so, in the therapy sessions with the psychiatrist there was never any mention of my mother being narcissistic. Nor did the psychiatrist ever suggest there was anything wrong with my mother. Toward the end of the six years of counseling he did say to me one day, "Susan, your mother is dead. Let go of her."

When I was twenty-six I married Dean. He was twenty-five, handsome, charming, college-educated, and becoming a hard-driving, successful business man. We were married for twenty-one years, although my midlife crisis began about five years before we divorced. During the midlife crisis, with the help of a competent marriage counselor who was willing to see me for four years even though Dean would not attend the sessions with me, I came to understand I had married a highly narcissistic man. And after being exactly who Dean wanted me to be for so many years, I began to resent his controlling ways, his manipulation of me, and the incessant prioritizing of his work over me and us. I became aware our relationship was a one-way street...with me doing all of the giving as I strove to be Dean's perfect wife.

Interestingly, the precipitating factor for both the midlife crisis and the divorce was a job change I made. After twelve years as a teacher in the public schools, I started taking summer and evening college courses in technology and business. This enabled me to find a new career in corporate America where I quickly became respected and valued. I also became increasingly aware of how differently, and how much better, I was being treated by the men at work than by my husband at home. As my self-respect and personal identity grew at work, I began to need changes in the marriage at home. Dean, however, didn't want changes. He wouldn't consider them. He wanted our former circumstances to continue. I needed to change and become my authentic self in all aspects of my life. That was not acceptable to Dean.

As this memoir begins I am spending several nights at the home of my dear friend, Penny. I want to be away from Dean and think about what needs to happen next in our marriage. It is five months before our 20th wedding anniversary. I am staying in Penny's lower-level recreation room where there is a ping pong table, two futons, and a bathroom with a shower. It is early evening as I take a small notebook out of my briefcase to write down my thoughts and feelings, hoping to gain more clarity about what to do. Little do I know as I start to write in the notebook, the practice of writing down my thoughts and feelings will become invaluable to me, helping me discern and understand what happened in the past, what is happening in the present, and what needs to happen in the future in order for me to facilitate the life-enhancing changes I so desperately need.

February 9, 1991

How do I feel now? I'm sooo tired. I'm tired of processing, tired of struggling.

Over the past ten days, several important thoughts have crystallized for me:

— I no longer have hope that Dean's and my marriage can be acceptable in the future.
— I think our relationship is unhealthy, destructive, and dangerous.
— Over the past week I've experienced an internal tug-of-war. I equate it to an addiction. I know the addictive substance (our relationship) is bad for me, but it is so hard to resist. I don't want to go home or be around Dean; but, really severing the relationship is not something I can do yet. I don't feel strong enough or comfortable enough with the permanency of that option.
— I don't want to be a divorced person. Being divorced goes against the grain of what I value, practice, and believe. I view divorced people as failures at some level. I don't view a divorced couple as having just a failed relationship. I also view them as individuals who have failed in one of life's most important endeavors. I guess for me it is the most important endeavor - because I have no children.

So here I am not wanting to be a divorced person, but also not wanting to be in what I think is an unhealthy relationship. And at the same time, I truly don't want to hurt Dean by leaving him.

In two days I will move into a furnished apartment with a thirty-day lease. I know I need more time away from Dean to think about our future together...or not together. I hate the step the move represents...possibly becoming "separated."

I don't really want to be alone. But I can't go home right now. That option feels wrong to me. And, I have decided I must not stay at Penny's much longer either. She and her family are so dear, but I must learn to be my own family now.

1

February 13, 1991
I saw the marriage counselor (Joe) today.

— He told me it isn't wrong to tell Dean what I think. He said, "You have moved out and Dean is entitled to know why."
— I told Joe about my recent phone conversation with Dean which ended in Dean hanging up on me. Joe said Dean's reaction is typical of the duality in his personality, and that duality causes me to be afraid. Joe commented that one minute Dean is very charming, and the next minute he is not - that Dean's narcissistic tendencies cause him to react to protect himself from hurt, and I suffer the erratic consequences. (I had never heard the word "narcissistic" before today. I had to look it up to be able to spell it and write it here.)
— Joe talked about Dean's constant need to control situations. I shared Dean's comment, "Couples have been working out their problems for hundreds of years and marriage counselors have only been around for twenty years." Joe responded, "When it is working for couples to talk their problems through in private that is fine. When it isn't working that is different." He explained it's a matter of roles. I need to be the patient with the problem; I don't need to be Dean's counselor. I agree with Joe…but Dean refuses to go to a counselor with me.
— I told Joe there is a part of me which believes Dean and I will never be able to have a relationship which feels right. On the other hand, I can't seem to let go of the relationship. Joe explained that I feel both ways at once due to Dean's dualistic, un-integrated personality which is exhibited in his two kinds of behavior toward me. Finally, that concept registered in my brain. It helped me understand why I feel I'm being pulled apart. I told Joe I cry all the time and am so upset and emotionally unstable I wonder if I am mentally ill. For the first time since I started seeing Joe, he actually smiled and laughed. He said I am not mentally ill, that I am going through one of the most stressful situations a human being can go through. He

said separation is right up there as number two or three of the top stressors – that pilots are not allowed to fly at a stress level of 70 and separation alone rates at 50.

Sigh…

I am in the apartment now. It is comfortable, bright and cheery. I have everything I need. It is quiet and I feel safe.

I am concerned about telling Dean I am going to visit my relatives this weekend. I am afraid it will create embarrassment for him. After talking to my brother yesterday, I realized he doesn't want his son to know Dean and I are having trouble. I understand that. On the other hand, if I need to put on a front with my family, maybe it isn't worth going. I guess I was hoping to get support from my brother, my stepmother, my step aunt, and maybe my nephew. Perhaps I'll change my mind and not go. It could be like Christmas again - hurting inside with the added stress of covering up. I don't need that.

February 16, 1991
This morning I decided to be positive. I put little yellow Post-its around the apartment. They say "Be positive."

Joe suggested I keep the lines of communication open with Dean but see him only in public places. So I called him yesterday and asked him if he would like to go to the movies together tonight. He said "yes" and I was looking forward to it. I got the tickets this afternoon and called to tell him the timing. He sounded abrupt and not thrilled about going out together. I felt so disappointed I decided to call him back and ask him if he <u>wanted</u> to go. He said "sure." I feel empty and sad. I was making an effort to be excited about tonight, and he just sounds like "ho-hum." Darn him.

(Later)

Oh my…I just realized something. I bet Joe told me to only see Dean in public places because a while ago I shared with him a bizarre experience I had with Dean. We had gotten into bed one night and I told Dean I wanted to talk with him about something. He responded, "Turn off the lamp and go to sleep." But I needed to talk to him then and I said, "Dean, I need to talk with you now." In a very demanding tone of voice he repeated, "Turn off the lamp and go to sleep." I felt very frustrated. So I decided to go downstairs to the family room since I knew I wasn't going to be able to go to sleep right away. I left the bedroom without turning the lamp off. As I got halfway down the stairs Dean yelled, "Come back here and turn that lamp off." That made me angry. I kept on going. When I got to the family room I sat down on the sofa and pulled the afghan around my shoulders.

In a few minutes Dean appeared in the doorway and growled at me, "Go upstairs and turn that lamp off." I looked at him and simply said, "No." He turned around, went into the kitchen, opened the door to the basement and went down the stairs. Shortly I heard him go back upstairs to the bedroom. And suddenly there was a loud sound of shattering glass. I ran up the stairs. Dean had smashed the lamp with a hammer he had gotten from his workbench in the basement. He was back in bed with his eyes closed. I decided to go back downstairs and stay in the family room all night. The next morning after Dean left for work, I went upstairs and cleaned up the debris. On my way home from work I bought a new lamp and then put it in place before Dean got home. We never spoke about the incident. Life went on as if it had never happened.

When I told Joe about this incident he quietly said, "You're lucky Dean didn't smash your head with that hammer." Sigh…

February 17, 1991

I hope Dean is going to grow now. Last night he was pleasant but strangely quiet. After the movie we sat in my car and I asked him how he was. At first he said he was okay. Then he said, "I'm a little depressed." I tried to get him to talk to me about it. He didn't seem to know whether to, or how to. I asked him to tell me what he was thinking. I patted his chest and asked, "What's going on in there?" No answer. I asked him if he was sad about us. He said, "I don't know where I am." I suggested he could talk with me about how he feels. But then it seemed like it was time to go. I told him I love him and kissed him. He said "I'll call you tomorrow," and I was obviously glad.

He was very polite during the evening. He warmed my car after the movie and asked if I'd be okay driving back to the apartment. Maybe I should go back home and give our marriage another try. Maybe Dean is finally in a place to become more introspective, considerate, and kind.

July 1, 1991

A lot has happened since I last wrote (four and a half months ago!). I moved back home with Dean after spending just ten days in the apartment. I decided I wanted to give our marriage another try since Dean seemed to be kinder to me. During the past four and a half months, it seemed like a lot of growth was taking place in our marriage. But tonight I need to write again because I want to figure out what just happened.

At dinner I mentioned to Dean I went shopping after work and bought a new suit and blouse. I told him I wasn't even excited about buying the new clothes because I am burned out from work and I am wanting to change from working full-time to part-time. He asked how much I spent on the clothes. I told him. He responded by saying that buying the clothes was the wrong thing to do if I am going to quit working full-time. He told me I won't be able to go shopping if I work less than full-time. That made me mad. We have quite enough money, and he is the one who is choosing to not work now. I dared to tell him I most certainly will go shopping if I want to.

Then he seemed to go back to a familiar behavior which I have just recently recognized - trying to scare me out of doing something. This time it didn't work. I was so angry I continued to stand up for myself. I reminded him I am not going to quit working; I just need to work less - say thirty hours a week. He then went off on a rant about <u>me</u> having to change my lifestyle. Next he said, "When I enforce the new budget…" and I interrupted him to say a new budget would need to be a "we" proposition. He ignored my words. Then I asked, "What about the two new cars and all the other things you bought after you sold your company and stopped working?" He had no response. I just looked at him and glared. Finally he said, "Maybe you're right. I shouldn't expect you to live within a budget that isn't in place yet." He got up from the table and turned on the TV. I did the dishes and came up to bed.

I am so disappointed. I am in desperate need of working less. I'm having strange tension headaches in the back of my head. I have waves of depression and have made an appointment with a different therapist because Dean said the marriage counselor I have been seeing isn't doing me any good and I need help.

How can he threaten me saying I can't buy what I want and need when I will still be making substantial money and we have plenty of money in our investment portfolio? He is the one who has taken a year off work - not me! This kind of thing makes me question whether we will stay together. He is just not who I want now, in so many ways. Why do I keep hanging on?

I certainly will cut back on my hours. But after this evening, I don't think I will continue to endorse my paychecks over to him while he gives me an allowance. I need to have my own nest egg just in case.

Boy, did I ever do the wrong thing when I married Dean! I'm sick of trying to make this marriage work. I think I'll quit trying. If he makes it work, fine. Otherwise, I'm out of here. I'm too old to share my precious years left on this earth with such a jerk. He's an intelligent and capable man, but he's a jerk in many important ways.

July 14, 1991

So much has happened in the last two weeks. Writing about it seems <u>overwhelming</u>; yet, I want to try to do it.

My decision to get out of the marriage came after a miserable July 4th weekend with good friends who live a day-trip away. Dean was rude to me during the entire trip. He refused to talk to me on the way there and whenever the two of us were alone. Finally on the way home, I had had enough. I told him we needed to have a serious talk when we got home. He said he didn't have time to talk to me. I responded, "Then we'll talk over dinner."

At dinner I began by saying, "You are not respecting my needs." Dean shot right back, "I don't respect you. I think you're a space shot." In the moment following that statement I thought to myself, "Then why am I still here?" That night I slept in the guest bedroom.

Over the next five days, I pondered what to do. Our 20th wedding anniversary was in the middle of that week, and I had planned a week's vacation for us to celebrate the event by traveling to the location where we had spent our honeymoon. But at the last minute, Dean said he didn't want to go - that I wasn't any fun. So I canceled the reservations and put aside the new lingerie I had bought for the occasion. Then I decided to still take the week off from work in order to figure out how to file for a divorce. On our 20th wedding anniversary, I secretly went to a lawyer and filed. My friend Jane had recommended the lawyer, and another friend, Evelyn, went with me to meet with the lawyer. The lawyer suggested a Restraining Order be placed on the joint investment portfolio Dean and I have. This means no money can be taken out of the account although normal trading can continue. I was surprised the lawyer suggested a Restraining Order. That seemed a little severe to me. But I agreed to it, deciding the lawyer probably knew best. Then the lawyer told me Dean would be served the divorce papers by a sheriff in two days. She also said the sheriff would need to have a witness with him when he served the papers.

I knew I couldn't bear to be the witness, so I asked a dear older friend and former neighbor, Donna, if she would be the witness. To my great relief she said "yes." I arranged to meet the sheriff on a street near my house and have Donna with me. When the sheriff drove up, Donna got into the sheriff's car with a baseball cap pulled down over her face so Dean could not recognize her. She and the sheriff drove off to serve Dean the divorce papers.

I was a nervous wreck as I sat in my car sobbing and waiting for Donna and the sheriff to return. As I was sobbing an image came into my mind which truly startled me. The image was one of an umbilical cord being cut. I sobbed more and more uncontrollably. When the sheriff and Donna returned, I could barely thank the sheriff because I was so upset. Donna got into my car and I started to drive back to her home where I was going to spend the night. About fifty yards down the road I became so dizzy I couldn't drive. I pulled off the road and sobbed and sobbed and sobbed some more. It seemed like a very long time until I could drive again, very slowly, to Donna's home.

The next morning I went back to our house. Dean was there. We went into the family room and sat opposite each other at the small table. He had obviously given considerable thought to what he wanted to say to me. He said a number of things:

— You destroyed 20 years of trust in one action.
— The action was hostile. It is an example of how the lawyers will escalate this thing. It will take on a life of its own. The normal way to do this is to talk about it and go together to be served at a lawyer's office. We are talking amicably now but we won't be soon.
— When I was served the divorce papers, I was angry at first. I thought I didn't deserve them. Now I realize I am not meeting your needs and I need to change some things. I talked to a therapist and want you to go with me to see him for counseling. He sounds very calm, like he has his head screwed on right. But if we

go to counseling, I want to come out of it with a mature, stable, middle-aged woman.
— I talked to your brother on the phone and asked him to come here to mediate our problems.
— I assume you don't want to try to reconcile.
— What do you want? The house? The car? What?

I answered his questions by simply saying, "I want a divorce." He scowled at me and got up from the table. There was no more discussion. I went upstairs to the guest bedroom. My lawyer had told me to stay in the house rather than move out. I decided to try to live mostly in the guest bedroom until the divorce is final.

Sigh…

July 20, 1991
I feel sad this morning. I'm ending my marriage - the one thing I prioritized above all else. I didn't want it to be like this. I wanted to live happily ever after. But I chose the wrong partner to make my dream come true.

I am not perfect, but I am willing to try almost anything to make things work out - anything except live with a man whose values about people and life are full of hate and anger and defensiveness. I feel so sorry for Dean; yet in twenty years of marriage he has not embraced the positive power of love, the joy of giving, or the ability to respect nice people.

He lives a defensive lifestyle and his words demonstrate this. "Cut people's throats from the inside out so they don't even know they are bleeding." "It's a game of inches." "The trick is making it look easy." He plans and plans and plans his financial stability. His sense of well-being is dependent on having control. He wants to be financially richer, but he's not generous to me or friends or family.

He is a person "of the lie" as Dr. M. Scott Peck describes in his book, *People of the Lie*. Dr. Peck says people of the lie seem to lack any motivation to be good, yet they intensely desire to appear good. Their goodness is all on a level of pretense and, in effect, a lie. Yet in reality their lie is not so much to deceive others as to deceive themselves because they cannot, or will not, tolerate the pain of self-reproach.

Dean is not a compassionate person. He is a selfish, emotionally sick person who doesn't want to change. And because Dean is a person of the lie, I am suffering. I am constrained from being who I really am. I can't love him and be loved by him in the way God would want, nor the way I want. The erratic mistreatment and verbal abuse are damaging me emotionally and physically. I am realizing I must have more self-respect than to let this other human being abuse me.

As difficult as it is to let go of my dream, our marriage must be finished. It is not a marriage of love and respect and caring. I will be infinitely better off to be alone, to learn who I am, and to build a loving family of friends. I beg your forgiveness, God, as I break my marriage vows. I entered into them with full commitment and have tried my very best to make the marriage work. I must take another path now.

July 27, 1991

Last night and this morning I'm not doing so well. Yesterday I was told by my lawyer's assistant that Dean was served a contempt of court summons because he illegally moved the entire contents of our joint investment portfolio account (of 20 years) into another account with only his name on it. I pictured him in my mind receiving the summons and felt physically sick to my stomach. It's as if I feel the pain for him.

I am feeling weak, God, weak because I do not have enough confidence in my own thoughts. I seem to always need verification of them. And yet there is a part of me which is trying so hard to believe in myself and get free from my addiction to Dean.

Oh God, please make me strong - strong in the right ways. Help me to believe what is right. Help me to know Your will in all of this. I think I know, but I am not used to making my own decisions and feeling sure of myself. Yet, I rejoice because I am freer now by filing for divorce and making plans to get physically away from Dean.

July 31, 1991

Oh God, what an awful day this was. I went to court with my lawyer, and Dean was there alone to represent himself in the contempt of court charge. He refuses to get a lawyer because he doesn't want to incur any legal expense.

My lawyer and Dean really got into it. He went off on a big tirade about the most important thing to him is keeping his career integrity. He said this when my lawyer requested the money be moved back into the joint account and frozen. He pleaded with the judge to consider what would happen to his career if this request were granted. He was perspiring and his hands were shaking. He looked like he could explode. It's the first time I have ever seen him in a situation he couldn't control. It made me feel guilt and pity and pain to see him in such a mess. I empathized with his total lack of control in the situation, his anger, and his frustration. He was beaten by my lawyer. He was just plain beaten. And his arguments, which he obviously believed in, fell on deaf ears. I felt so badly for him. My lawyer was strong and stood up to him well.

At the beginning of the hearing Dean said he was totally taken by surprise at the divorce complaint - that he wanted to reconcile. He said he moved the money because he feared I would write a check and the money would be gone. Good grief! The reality is that I have never had a check book for our stock and bond portfolio, nor have I ever accessed the account to buy and sell stocks or bonds. Sigh…My lawyer countered Dean on every move. The judge went with her.

I managed to hold up in the courtroom but I think I must have been in a state of shock after my lawyer and I exited the courthouse. She looked at me and said, "Why aren't you smiling? We won!" I responded, "I guess I just need some time to process what happened." She said with frustration, "There's nothing to process, Susan. We won!" I nodded and walked off in a daze to find my car. On the way home I had to pull off the busy highway because I felt so anxious and upset I couldn't drive. Finally, when I was able to drive again, I drove straight to Penny's house and collapsed in her arms.

How can I break my allegiance, caring, and empathizing with Dean? I feel so badly for him…but he isn't feeling badly for me…Whatever will he do?

Oh God, I have made my choice to leave Dean. Perhaps I should have told him first before I filled for the divorce - but surely he would have moved the money anyway and tried to manipulate me for his advantage. I can't go on and make this divorce a success if I don't learn how to break away from his brainwashing and his unhealthy hold on my emotions.

Please help me, God. I don't know how to break away. I know I must - but I don't know how.

August 3, 1991
Today was a tough day. I moved into a small furnished apartment located halfway between my home with Dean and where I work. Contrary to my lawyer's suggestion, I figured out I couldn't tolerate staying in the house with Dean until the divorce is final. I feel better now that I am no longer living in the same house with him, but moving into this tiny apartment

seems like I am on a business trip in a less than desirable location. And I know I may be here for quite a few months until the divorce is final.

Sigh...

August 6, 1991

I liked what my minister said when I went to talk with him today. He said he thought I was "courageous" to file for the divorce - and for the way I did it. He didn't think I was bad for filing in secret. And he thinks my concern about breaking my marriage vows is inappropriate too. He doesn't think God wants us to be unhappy, and he thinks Dean broke the vows first by the way he acted toward me. He also suggested that when I now feel sad instead of angry at Dean, it is because I wasn't allowed to be angry at Dean – that a pattern existed in which I was allowed to be sad and remorseful with Dean but not angry. And now that sad feeling connects me to Dean whereas anger will separate me from him.

My minister also prayed with me. One of the things he prayed for was courage for me. He also prayed for God's grace to take away my guilt. And he prayed for Dean too. I am VERY grateful for my minister...for his counsel and his prayers.

September 4, 1991

Oh dear...Oh dear...Oh dear. Today I had an annual physical with my PCP. The last part of the physical was a pelvic exam. I positioned myself in the stirrups and the doctor started the procedure. Very soon he exclaimed, "You have vaginal warts!" Confused, frightened and unfamiliar with his terminology I immediately asked, "What is that?" He stood up, looked at me with obvious disdain and said, "It is a sexually transmitted disease." I looked at him in shock for a few moments and then managed to say, "But I have never been with anyone but my husband." He continued to look at me judgmentally, clearly not believing me. Then he spoke again, "You will have to find a gynecologist to treat you for this STD." I felt overwhelmed. I still do. I will need to find a gynecologist tomorrow and schedule an appointment to be treated for vaginal warts. How can this be happening?

September 11, 1991

Today I went to a gynecologist whom a work friend recommended. I liked him. He treated the warts by applying acid to them. The treatment hurt like HELL! And I will need to go back for more painful treatments over several months. (Sigh)

The good news is that the doctor is a kind and compassionate man. He heard my story before examining me and then stayed with me after the treatment until my physical pain and anxiety began to subside.

This whole situation seems so unreal to me. (Tears)

October 17, 1991

I went back to the house today to get some of my things I need for the fall. I took my friend Carol with me. Dean let us in and followed me around, glaring while I got my winter clothes together. There was a workman in the garage whom I know. He was one of Dean's former employees and is helping Dean build a new front walk.

Carol helped me carry things out to my car. Then at one point she was outside and I was upstairs with Dean. I went to the linen closet to get the old, twin-size electric blanket. Dean said I couldn't take it. I looked at him with a frown on my face and told him I need it because it is cold in my apartment. "Besides," I continued, "the king-size electric blanket is there for you." I started down the stairs and he followed me saying, "If you take that blanket, I will disable your car and you won't be able to leave." Amazingly, I didn't let him intimidate me. I ignored him and put the blanket in my car. When I took the next load of my clothes to the car, I noticed the blanket was gone. As I went back into the house, it occurred to me Dean would have hidden the blanket in his office closet. I went to the closet and there it was. I stuffed it in one of the trash bags I had brought to carry clothes in and quietly put it back in my car. When I was ready to leave, I went back into the garage. Dean, his former employee, and Carol were there. Dean told me I had better bring that blanket back into the house before I left. Then I did something I have never, ever done before. In front of other people, I raised my voice, disagreed with Dean, and stood up to him. I told him he was being ridiculous, that I needed a blanket to keep myself warm and I was not walking off with a family heirloom. He said he would call my attorney. I said that was fine with me. Carol and I got into my car and drove off.

I was shaken but felt justified in my actions. Then I felt bad for Dean because I know how excruciatingly painful it was for him to have someone else witness my standing up to him. Never ever in front of others have I disagreed with him. That wasn't allowed in public, or in private for that matter. I'm sure he was shaken too. The reality is - as in so many other situations I never challenged throughout the years – Dean's position <u>was</u> ridiculous.

November 11, 1991
Dean is trying to destroy me with his lies - his lies which are meant to cripple me emotionally. I must shield myself from his emotional assault and remember I am <u>not</u> weak emotionally. I am strong and I'm getting stronger. I know the truth about why I don't have a child; I know the actual facts.

I just read Dean's written response to the interrogatories my lawyer sent to him. He wrote that he saved all his life to have children, and he wants the court to award him the monies to have children and educate them in his next marriage. When I read those words I physically felt a pain in my heart – like a sword piercing it. I thought I might be having a heart attack.

The truth is very different. Two years after we were married, Dean told me he didn't want to have children because he was "not willing to invest the time and money children would require." Then four years ago, I finally figured out I really wanted to be a parent. And because my tubes had been permanently tied years before, I knew I would need to use in vitro fertilization (IVF) to get pregnant. So I researched IVF, and when I had completed my research I made a special dinner for Dean and me one evening. During the dinner I told him I wanted to become a parent, we could do it using in vitro fertilization, and the health insurance from my job would pay for it. Much to my surprise and delight, Dean agreed to my request. When I reflected on his response later, I decided he must have imagined he could handle becoming a parent at that time because the company he had started a few years earlier looked like it would be successful.

I tried the in vitro process three times. The first two times I didn't get to the fertilization procedure because the hormones I was prescribed didn't cause my body to produce multiple eggs. The third time I did get to the fertilization procedure but only one of three eggs turned out to be viable, and that egg and Dean's sperm didn't unite. After that third try I knew I should not try again – based on my age and the effects I had felt from having so many extra hormones in my body for the IVF procedures.

I understand the despicable mind-game Dean is trying to play with his response to the interrogatories. His tactic caught me off guard and upset me at first, but now I must make some choices. I can let his attack scare and confuse me or I can see it for what it is – a lie - and look beyond it to define what it means. It means Dean is a desperate man. He is desperate to defend his "exemplary" performance in the marriage. He is desperate to justify why his marriage didn't produce children. He is desperate to preserve the material assets of the marriage for himself. What is so very sad is the possibility that deep down inside him - or maybe not so deep down inside him now but very near the surface - he realizes he failed miserably in the things in life which are truly important. He succeeded to a degree in obtaining material things but he neglected all else. What a sad story.

What is done is done. It cannot be changed. There is only the future to deal with. How shall I deal with it to make it rich in meaning and memories? God, I need Your help on this. I want so much to make the next period in my life meaningful. To do that, I must end this period well and put my sights on a better life ahead.

December 3, 1991
Today was a turning point day…a happy, growth day…a day when I took a giant leap toward becoming my own person and putting the past behind me.

Yesterday Dean, his lawyer, my lawyer, and I met. The meeting was business-like and each of the four of us spoke our minds on things. Dean presented two settlement proposals. Both were based on my getting 50% of the house equity, 30% of the assets and 0% of a significant business endeavor Dean put together a few months before I filed for divorce. My lawyer was receptive to the format. I watched Dean do his negotiating dance.

Then this morning when I was getting ready for work, I had a major revelation. I realized the best thing to do now is to tell my lawyer I don't want to negotiate anymore. I want to take this divorce to court. I realized that for twenty years Dean has manipulated me and negotiated with me, and I have lost over and over again playing by his rules. Now I realize I don't have to play by his rules anymore. I am going to choose not to play the game - the negotiation game. I am not going to let him negotiate the most important financial settlement of his life - at least not without a third party's assistance. And that third party will be a judge.

I am in no hurry now. I am comfortable in my new apartment and I have plenty of money to live on from my paycheck.

So my terms are 50% of everything including the business deal, and I am not willing to consider anything less. This is my first and last offer. I also decided to refuse Dean's request to continue his healthcare benefits through the company which employs me. I provided him with the COBRA forms - he can pay his own way.

I am truly ready now to get on with my life. I feel wonderfully okay. Okay that it's possible to be a nice person and still say "no" to Dean's wants. Okay to really make the break. Okay and excited about what's before me in life (without Dean).

The struggle is over emotionally for me. I give You thanks, God. And I invite You to guide and protect me as I chart a new course. I am learning to be there for myself. I am learning that life is, and can be, so much better without Dean. He is a sorry soul. I pity him and I wish him well, but I will no longer care for him or cover up for him. It is done and I am ready to move on.

December 8, 1991
The divorce is final! After I chose to determine the divorce settlement in court, Dean – via his lawyer – offered a cash settlement amount. It was definitely not equivalent to 50% of all we have. It was, however, quite enough for me. I accepted it. I am thrilled. Case closed. Onward!

January 5, 1992
Over the past year I experienced great pain and confusion. Now I am feeling great joy. This joy is a wonderful, sustaining, spiritual joy. It is a joy of peace and acceptance. It is a joy of dispelled fear. It is a joy of centeredness and gratitude. It is a joy of great love.

I had many talks with God throughout the past year, and I have come to rely on those talks. They help me know my own mind. They bring me insights. And more recently they have caused me to feel loved by God, to feel God loves me personally and is always available to me. I have but to ask Him to be with me. And for the first time in my life I feel truly secure. Secure, and loved, and not alone, and not afraid. "Not afraid." Those words are so meaningful to me. I think I have been afraid all of my life. And now I don't have to be afraid anymore. Hallelujah!

February 17, 1992

I have met a wonderful man. His name is Michael. We are falling in love. Our attraction to each other is physical, emotional, spiritual, and intellectual. I believe he has a great capacity to love. The attraction is so strong, it is leaving me reeling. He says he feels obsessed with me. I feel similarly with him. It's magical. It's stimulating. It's exhausting.

My concern tonight is the emotional stress I am experiencing. Somehow the exhilaration I feel must be tempered. It is so strong it is keeping me from sleeping well and concentrating. My body is showing signs of fatigue and frayed nerves. I want to be able to relax with Michael. I don't want to "perform" when I'm with him. I want to love him and be loved by him. I want to be myself with him - more than I ever was with Dean. I want to feel comfortable with Michael.

Now I want to remember how my relationship with Michael started. In late January I was assigned at work to a short, out-of-town project with a man from another office location in a nearby town. We began to get to know each other on the plane ride to the client's site. After we finished preparing for the client visit, Michael asked me what my aspirations are regarding the company. I told him I hadn't really thought about it much – that I was currently focused on going through a major transition in my life. He asked what the transition is. I told him it is a divorce. To my surprise, he became very interested in what is going on with me. I told him just a little about it and then he looked away for a few moments. When he turned back to face me again he told me he had been married for almost thirty years and he hadn't been happy for the past fifteen. I nodded in response - to acknowledge I had heard what he said.

We spent several days at the client site working together. Our time together was productive, collaborative, and fun. When we arrived back at our home airport, he walked me to my car in the airport parking garage. When he said goodbye he leaned over and kissed me on the cheek. Over the next two weeks we got together several times to do the follow-up work for the client we had visited. Those times were also productive, collaborative, and fun. It would be accurate to say we became very smitten with each other right away.

February 25, 1992

I received a very long letter from Michael today. He wrote about many things including the following thoughts and feelings about me:

— In his entire life he has not known a woman with my qualities - funny, sexy, sensuous, intelligent, and beautiful in every way.
— Just thinking about me arouses and stimulates him.
— He thinks about me all the time and wants to be in touch with me frequently.
— He needs me as a friend but wants me as a lover.

And he wrote the following thoughts and feelings about himself:

— He is a mess and has been for a long time. His marriage has not been a happy one for 15 years, and he has - to date - avoided confronting his wife. It's time for him to square that away.
— He's not certain what his personal values and goals are because he has for so long tried to meet the image demanded by society, family, jobs, and himself. He has finally - he hopes - reached a point where he will pursue and find that being and image he wants to become. It may be an itinerant sailor, a Harley rider, a home builder, or a businessman. He suspects a bit of all, but until he knows he cannot offer much to anyone, including himself.

— Knowing me has given him the conviction to face the long-standing problem of his marriage…he just didn't have any idea how much it was going to hurt.

— He loves me and prays things will work out so we can be together.

Oh my goodness…this is a lot to take in.

March 2, 1992

Last week I shared with Michael how confusing and agonizing it was for me to make the decision to leave Dean. I also told him I went to a marriage counselor off-and-on for four years - by myself, because Dean refused to go with me. Michael just told me he has found a therapist for himself and another for his wife. He has decided they will both see separate therapists for a year and then they will see a marriage counselor together.

I feel terrible – disappointed Michael isn't ready to choose me, ashamed I let myself fall in love with a married man, and very regretful I have caused so much pain for Michael, his wife, and their family. I guess I am learning a lesson which a great many women have learned - don't fall in love with a married man. It's time for me to put the brakes on and stop our relationship. This is not a game I can play. I will not date a married man while he and his wife are going to separate therapists with the expectation that a year from now they will see a marriage counselor together. Michael's decision to stay with his wife or leave her must be made without my seeing him or influencing him in any way. I am NOT a home-wrecker.

Sigh…Our relationship has been so sweet. Michael has loved me in a way I have longed to be loved for my entire life. It feels to me like he is <u>the</u> love of my life. Love flows out of me to him and back into me from him, like the motion of the infinity symbol – back and forth, back and forth, surrounding us, and filling both of us up to overflowing with joy…Sigh… But now it must be over. I feel sad, very sad and very disappointed. If only Michael were further along in his identity crisis.

March 15, 1992

I'm realizing I have work to do alone in order to define who I am. The work will include selecting a home for myself and buying it. It will include discovering what my tastes are and furnishing my home. It will include selecting activities for my life which have meaning to me. And when I know what my own tastes are…and when I have figured out what gives me pleasure in life as well as what I can give to life…and when I have learned how to care for myself spiritually, emotionally, physically, and financially, then and only then will I be ready to be with a man in a partnership.

I am feeling anxious now because part of me wants to support Michael at this difficult time in his life, while part of me is fearful of being in a supportive role - fearful because I do not want to influence Michael's decision to get or not get a divorce. If I were just his friend, I could play a supportive role; but I feel very tense about playing that role when I am in love with him. It's too much for me. I can't handle it.

So, what will I do?

I honestly don't think I can stop loving Michael. I'm too in love with him to do that. I wonder if I can share other troubling parts of his life with him but not the details of his separation and divorce from his wife. I want to date Michael, but I can't do it until he is at least separated from his wife. What we're doing now is wrong. Seeing each other is unfair to me, to him, and to his wife. Should we completely stop our communication until he moves out and calls me? Or should we allow ourselves to talk on the phone but no more voicemails?

The ideal situation for me short-term will be to stop all communication with him and take care of myself without him in the picture. The ideal situation for me long-term will be to wait until Michael is separated and then date him for quite a long while from two separate households. Then, if and when it feels right, I will want to live with him…and maybe marry him some day.

Oh my…This situation is very complicated.

March 21, 1992

Last night I saw Michael to say goodbye - goodbye for what I hope is just a while. What an amazing seven weeks we have had. We have fallen in love and felt passion and desire and friendship, and respect, and caring, and great joy. And then I began to feel very anxious - almost phobic – and I finally realized I cannot participate in the relationship with Michael anymore until he is separated from his wife and filed for a divorce.

Of course, there's no way to know how long that will take, or if it will ever happen for that matter. He says he feels less and less to nothing for his wife now. He has put their house on the market because he's discussed it with her and neither of them wants to stay in the house if they break up. His wife has told her friends what is going on, and he has told some of his friends and one of his three sons. But he also says he doesn't know why he just can't leave yet – that he thinks he is getting ready to leave. He asked me if I will wait for him. I didn't answer the question. Instead, I told him I love him and if and when he is separated and filed for a divorce and wants to call me, to do so.

Dear God,
Please care for Michael. Guide and protect him. Grant him Your grace, Your wisdom, and Your peace. And please grant me Your grace and wisdom and peace too. Amen

March 24, 1992

Whew, I need to write. I spoke to Michael a bit ago - he called on the pretense of work stuff. And now I'm obsessed and crazy again. What is it? Why do I become so energized? I just go on emotional overload. I can't think clearly.

I asked him how he is. He replied by telling me several big things. He said he thinks I saved his life. And connected to that, he said there is something else he hopes to tell me sometime. (I can't imagine what that is and I am curious to know.) He said he thinks he'll send flowers to his wife's therapist.

I asked him why. He said the therapist told his wife it sounds like he is ready to move on and she should begin to get on with her life.

He mentioned he had a good session with his therapist. And he said he misses me, loves me, and his feelings for me are getting stronger not weaker. He asked me how I am doing. I don't remember exactly what I replied. I think I told him I miss him and I believe what we are doing is the right thing to do. He said to let him know if I decide we can have some level of communication.

It is so difficult for me to resist Michael.

April 14, 1992

I have been in NYC on a work assignment this week. And it turned out Michael travelled to NYC to meet with a client yesterday. So we planned an evening together last night. We had a lovely, romantic dinner at a French restaurant, went to see the musical CATS, had a drink afterward, and parted at the elevator in the hotel where we stayed in separate rooms. It was a magical, beautiful evening together. I will never forget Michael taking my hand and looking into my eyes during a love song sung by the cast of CATS.

He left me a voicemail early this morning. It began, "Good Morning, Darling." He then went on to say he just doesn't know what memory he has that is more pleasant than last night's – that the moments he spends with me are so wonderful, he hasn't the words to describe them. He said he can't be apart from me…he's got to do something. It's not fair to me and it's not fair to him.

He ended the voicemail saying it was absolutely joyous last night…a troubled few hours afterwards…but he guesses it is his turn to be really anxious…and he is anxious for us. He doesn't ever want to have to walk away from me again like he did at the end of the evening last night. He said he loves me, and we'll connect sometime soon.

Sigh…

April 18, 1992
Today I received a beautiful bouquet of Easter flowers from Michael – including one single red rose. He wrote on the card, "You are the most love-filled and wonderful person I've ever had the fortune to meet. I hope this EASTER is a sort of resurrection for you. You deserve a new life filled with joy, smiles and warm memories. God bless you forever. Happy Easter, Michael"

Sigh…

April 20, 1992
Michael just told me his therapist said there was something wrong in his relationships as a child and until he knows what that is he will continue to have a string of unsuccessful relationships. Yikes! I feel very threatened by the therapist's words. Does this mean Michael can't have a successful relationship with me? Oh dear…

What Michael has told me about his relationship with his parents is that he was not consistently supported nor regarded by them as worthwhile and good. As incredible as that seems to me, he was cast in the role of the one responsible for screw-ups, and as the one unworthy of acceptance and love. I wonder if he has spent most of his life trying to be accepted and loved?

I think Michael is very worthy of acceptance and love, and I want him to regard himself as worthy of those things. He once said he feels almost "pure" with me. I suspect that's because I delight in Michael being Michael and I want to encourage him to be Michael. Authentic Michael is the man I love!

April 26, 1992
I really need to write. A lot has happened with Michael. This past week he seemed a bit distant. Today he called and we talked a long time - almost an hour. He admitted that last week he started to fall back into the old pattern

- thinking maybe it isn't so bad where he is. And he said he didn't know if I'd like it or not, but he really didn't think he could walk away from his situation if it weren't for me. I was feeling so in love with him, I was very understanding and supportive.

Then all of a sudden this afternoon I started to feel differently. What he said soaked in - that last week he felt like maybe it isn't so bad where he is. How can he say that after three months of getting to know me, saying he loves me, and telling me he wants to leave his wife? He is going through a tough time, but he's having his cake and eating it too. No, damn it, I've risked a lot to try out this relationship. Tonight I feel it's time to call a spade a spade. This is not fair to me. He's not being a man about this. He's not telling his wife he wants a divorce. Instead, he's telling her that she will have to change to be the woman he wants. And he tells me he loves me but can't bring himself to leave his wife. Based on today's conversation, I'm starting to lose respect for him. If he loves me and he wants out of his marriage, then he better be man enough to act on his convictions. I am feeling used, and thank you very much, I don't care to do "being used" anymore.

I need to tell Michael I am just not available until he gives me notice he is separated and filed for a divorce. I can't give anymore without some serious actions from him. I need to choose not to be used. Being compassionate is one thing. Investing in a relationship that's showing signs of stalling is stupid.

May 25, 1992

I received a letter from Michael today. He has been on vacation by himself for the past week. Some excerpts from his letter are:

— I was walking on the beach this morning thinking I fell in love with you nearly on day 1 of our business trip together…
— Whenever I think of you I smile – inside and out. I enjoy you in every way…

— You are right when you say we are a gift from God to each other...
— You make me feel it is okay to dream and to feel...in fact you encourage it by joining in...
— I can't even imagine wanting anything from a woman you couldn't provide. There is simply no need in me to think of anyone else...
— I'm learning about me again. I'm not half bad despite my nonconforming, rebellious nature. In fact, I never want to lose that side of me...
— While I am finding direction in some ways, I'm still troubled in others. Do I deserve this level of happiness (old neurosis)? If I leave the marriage can I do so knowing I did all I could to try to make it work? No answer yet. I take commitments rather seriously when I make them so that is an important answer for me to get.
— In my heart of hearts, I know that nothing I do will make me as happy as I am with you...

He signed the letter, "Know that you are missed, loved, wanted, appreciated, respected and cherished."

And a postscript said, "Not sure what's happening. I find I am extraordinarily emotional – I think I'm letting the 'blue suit control' dissipate and a lot of pent up stuff is coming through. God, what swings! I need to get control again!"

July 3, 1992
I wrote Michael the following letter and handed it to him at his office yesterday:

Dear Michael,
 My heart is breaking. I have never wanted to be with anyone as much as I want to be with you.

I feel your hurt. I feel your wife's hurt. I feel your family's hurt. I hurt so much for everyone involved, including myself, I can hardly stand it.

I have decided there is only one way to proceed now, and that way will hurt terribly too. But it is the only way I know to truly give you the freedom and space you need, and to remove me from the temptress and victim roles I feel I am in now.

I must let you go. I must not speak with you or see you until you have decided what you will do, and you have executed your decision. You may decide to go back to your wife and make it work - that your dream of a life-long marriage and your commitment to such a marriage are what count for you. Or, you may decide to end your marriage and your commitment to it - that you are ready to detach from your wife and build a new life without her. As long as you are somewhere between these decisions and their execution, we cannot be.

You know how much I care about you and want you, Michael. I will be empty without our sunshine. I know I will continue to think about you all the time just as I have for over five months. And I will pray with all of my heart that God will grant you, and your wife, and your family, His grace and wisdom and comfort.

Whatever you decide, my love, I will accept and understand.

Susan

Twenty-four hours later, I realize the last sentence in the letter is not a true statement for me. It is, instead, a statement which I thought Michael needed to hear – and a statement I thought I should put in the letter. In reality, I continue to believe Michael will most assuredly leave his wife and come to be with me. How could he not make that choice? Surely it is only a matter of time. His choosing otherwise would be unacceptable to me and impossible for me to understand. Oh my…At the end of the letter I didn't remain true to my authentic feelings. I went back to being who "the other" wanted me to be. Damn. I am so sorry I did that.

July 7, 1992

I received a letter from Michael today. He started the letter with the words, "Good morning my very dearest Susan." He said he had read my letter half a dozen times, and he became sadder each time he read it. He said he agrees with my decision...that one of us had to make it and he didn't have the resolve...he wanted me too much. He said that surprisingly, amid the sadness, he is also experiencing a sense of relief - from not having to meet a timetable to end his marriage. He said he must do all that he can to save his marriage in a timeframe which works for him and not one which works for me. He is sorry I feel like a victim...that I took him out of the shade and back into the sun. Toward the end of the letter he said, "God willing, we will be together again." He signed the letter, "Love always darling, Michael."

Michael's word "relief" in his letter bothers me a lot. It causes me to feel sickeningly uncomfortable. How can I cope, adapt, and survive this change in Michael's sentiments? I don't have an answer for that question.

July 22, 1992

I received a letter and book from Michael today. The book is titled *Principle-Centered Leadership*. The author is Stephen R. Covey. Mr. Covey was the guest speaker at a conference Michael recently attended.

Michael began his letter by saying his feelings of loss and emptiness about us are intensifying rather than diminishing. Then he wrote the following words, "Stephen Covey's basic premise is that in order to be whole, people and organizations need to operate at the principle rather than personality level. We need to be principle-centered to be happy, to make good decisions, to contribute to the world and so on. I find, upon self-examination, that I lost my principles over the years and also lost my way. Not only have you helped me begin to re-establish my principles, you have given me someone to know who is principle-centered---you - whom I both love and respect. I am going to do my damndest to become the type of man worthy of you. That is just one more gift you have given me, Susan."

Sigh…Didn't Michael and I just agree to not be in contact with each other? Why is resisting his words so difficult for me? I guess because I want to believe them so much.

July 27, 1992

Today I received a long letter from Michael. Toward the end of it he wrote the following: "I've already begun talking to my therapist about detachment. He said to do so I must deal more with feeling than thought. I will work hard on doing that. He, by the way, feels my relationship with you is stronger and truer than that at home. Time will tell."

Sigh…more hope-inducing words…

August 6, 1992

Wow - I am seething with anger. What a dope I've been, and how blind and naïve. But I'm nowhere near as angry at myself as I am at Michael. That lousy, low-life, irresponsible, weak, weak, weak man is a terrible excuse for a human being. Today at lunch time when I was sitting at a picnic table outside my office building, he drove up in his sports car, got out, and walked over to me. He said he came to my office location to give something to someone in the building and was hoping to see me. Then he stood there telling me how complete he feels with me…while at the same time wearing his wedding ring again. He hasn't had that on for weeks – at least not in my presence. Give me a break. Talk about feeling like a fool. I'm absolutely amazed and disgusted I let myself become so smitten with Mr. Slick. And then he called me later and told me I look better when I smile - that I should concentrate on trying to smile. Aargh!

Well, it hurts to arrive at this point, but my tolerance limit has been hit. He is a mess and I don't respect him. Under the guise of being an honest and open man, he betrays his principle to confront his marriage problem "properly" by running off at the mouth with words of unequaled love for me - which is, by the way, manipulation of me because he has no intention of taking actions to be with me. Ohhhhhhhhhhhhhhhhh...He makes me furious!!!

To think I dreamed of being this guy's lifetime lover and friend. To think I thought God sent him into my life and he would be the love of my life. How utterly blind and foolish I have been. I am ashamed, embarrassed, and disgusted.

August 31, 1992
Michael left me a voicemail today. He said he is missing me terribly - that he misses my touch, my thoughts, our talks, my smile. And then he said his recurring dream of a desert scene with a rose (himself) which was tightly shut for so many years and then opened up when he met me, is now closed again. He sounded in great pain, and a part of me wants to go to him and love him and hold him and tell him I love him and everything will be okay. But another part of me believes I must not respond to his voicemail. And as nice as it feels to know he is missing me, his lack of integrity is showing again. He's supposed to be trying to make things work with his wife, and he's leaving love messages for me. Of course I'm very, very sorry he is in pain, but I will not lack the integrity which this situation calls for from me.

October 19, 1992
Today I received a large envelope from Michael with a copy of Catherine Marshall's "Prayer of Relinquishment" in it. A note on a yellow Post-it said, "I liked this so I thought you might also. Hope you are well."

I read the prayer and it didn't resonate with me. It must have resonated a lot with Michael or he wouldn't have sent it to me. The essence of Catherine Marshall's prayer is about relinquishing what we want to have happen, in order to be able to receive and accept what God wants to have happen.

I suspect Michael is thinking he needs to relinquish our relationship in order to accept God's will that he not get a divorce.

Sigh...Michael's former phrase "time will tell" comes to mind.

November 17, 1992
I received a short letter from Michael today. He was writing from another out-of-state conference site. His opening salutation made me furious. He had the nerve to write, "Hi Jez." Then the letter included the following words, "I love you and will for the rest of my life. My difficulty is not in my emotion, but in trying to decide what is right. Right in my eyes and in God's. Simply wanting you as badly as I do is not enough, Susan, and I'm sorry that it's not that easy for me." He closed with, "Be well, love. I am always with you in thought if not body." And he signed his name as "Bozo."

Yes, he is a bozo! And I am <u>very</u> distraught and angry at him for addressing me as "Jez." How dare he use the name of the Biblical temptress Jezebel in the salutation of a letter to me! I don't think it's funny. I don't think it's clever. I think it is cruel beyond measure!!

December 30, 1992
I finally connected with my out-of-state, work friend, Bernice, who is also Michael's friend. She saw Michael over a week ago and has been dreading to tell me the news. He told her he is going to stay with his wife for another year or two. If they can get along, fine. He said they talked it over and agreed that if they both need to have affairs they will do so. My friend was shocked by his words and actually hit Michael as she told him she couldn't believe he would do to another person what he has done to me. He responded that in the future he will have affairs with married women, not single ones. He also told my friend it is different for him than for me.

That it isn't just leaving his wife; it is also leaving the fifty people in his family and his friends.

NOW I MUST LEARN THIS LESSON. I MUST BE VERY CAUTIOUS AND CAREFUL WHEN I GIVE MY LOVE TO SOMEONE. I MUST WATCH THE BEHAVIOR NOT JUST LISTEN TO THE WORDS OF ANY FUTURE BEAU. I'VE BEEN BADLY BURNED BECAUSE I HAVE NOT BEEN DISCERNING ENOUGH.

Yes, I am very angry and very hurt. I am also suffering from abandonment!

January 27, 1993
Today I received a card and flowers from Michael, including one single red rose. Today's date is the one year anniversary of our meeting on the business trip to a client site.

Michael wrote the following words on the card, "One year ago my life began a change that will impact me forever. I have had wonderful and unequaled pleasure, and some pain that is lasting longer than the pleasure. While the destination is still uncertain, I thank you for being the impetus for me to finally face the man in the mirror. The feelings remain. Michael"

There aren't words to express my despair at Michael continuing to send me letters which show the duality of his emotions.

February 23, 1993
Two days ago Michael saw me at work when he was in a meeting at my office location. Afterward he left me a voicemail which said, "In a simple short phrase, I miss you…terribly."

I responded by sending him a card with the following note inside:

"What did the voicemail mean?
1) Nothing has changed. You miss me but have made no decision.
2) You have decided to stay with your wife but still miss me.
3) You have decided to file for a divorce and are looking forward to our being able to see each other after you are separated and filed.

If 1 or 2 are true, please do <u>NOT</u> contact me in any way. To do so is to tease and manipulate me. I can't stand the pain."

Today I received a response from Michael in the mail. He said:

— My note to him was justified and the meaning of the voicemail was exactly what it said - no more, no less. Seeing me engendered feelings that led to his doing a selfish, thoughtless, weak thing. For that he is sorry. But, for me to assume that he was teasing and manipulating me is a great disappointment. How cruel do I think he is?

— With respect to my questions...There are days when he thinks he can make his marriage work and there are as many days when he is convinced it won't. He will continue to try until he makes a clear decision in one direction.

— And then he said...There has been one change which negates any chance of us ever being together. Before me, he had spent his adult life inside a protective circle. No one ever got through to him. No closeness - no hurt. No love - no loss. I got through and it was wonderful. Now it is not. All it has led to is pain for me, him, his wife and others. His original life of being closed was the right one for him. He will never again let anyone that near. So divorced or not, we will not have what we had and what I so richly deserve from someone. My request, therefore, for no personal contact will happen.

He ended the letter, "Good-bye, Susan. I wish you happiness and love. M."

I cried for 15 minutes after I read Michael's response. Then I thought about it a little more…and I decided his response was a "crock of _ _ _ _!"

March 10, 1993

I talked to Michael face-to-face for two hours today. I expressed my anger at his response to my previous note. Then I listened to his story - as a therapist would listen. His story has not changed…

April 5, 1993

Today I saw Michael at a company seminar and I attended a presentation he gave. After the seminar we spoke briefly regarding business matters only. There was no flirting by either of us. I missed that. I think Michael looks old, tired, lonely, sad, and broken. Sigh…Perhaps it makes sense he looks this way.

May 5, 1993

This afternoon I spoke on the phone with a work friend, Darlene, who knows Michael and me. She thinks Michael's commitment not to abandon his wife is as strong for him as my commitment not to have an affair with a married man. This simple explanation makes sense to me. I finally realize Michael's "trying to make the marriage work" is <u>not</u> the issue. Rather, divorce is not an option for Michael – as long as his wife wants to stay married to him.

August 1, 1993

I just learned about the concept of "codependency" from Darlene. She said a codependent relationship is a type of dysfunctional helping relationship in which a person supports or enables another person's addiction, poor mental health, immaturity, irresponsibility, or underdevelopment. She also said accomplishing detachment from a codependent relationship can require a lot of time. Wow! I don't remember ever hearing the word "codependency" before and now I am realizing I had codependent relationships with my mother and Dean. Oh dear...

It is clearly very important for me to read about and understand the concept of codependency. I need to know the symptoms of codependent relationships, the causes, and the cures. I suspect knowing about these things will help me a lot!

August 6, 1993

I called Michael today to ask him if he has decided to stay with his wife. I wanted to hear from him directly what his current thinking is.

He said he has decided to stay with her - that he isn't in love with her but things aren't bad enough to make him leave and family things like an upcoming wedding pull him back in. He told me they both went to therapists for a year and learned they are very different people who don't belong together. Then they went to a marriage counselor who said to Michael, "You have 30+ years invested in this marriage. Are you going to salvage it or not?" Michael decided he would salvage it - that while he doesn't feel good about the decision to stay, he does feel it is the "right" decision.

He said he thinks of me every day more than once. He asked how I am and I told him I didn't call to discuss that. He told me he's been avoiding my office location but we can't do that forever. I said we can try. I thanked him for telling me the answer to my question and hung up.

I hope I can learn to completely detach emotionally from Michael and I hope that detachment can come sooner rather than later. I do suspect it won't be easy for me. My history of emotional detachment has been infrequent and accomplished over years not months.

September 12, 1993

Several weeks ago Penny gave me the name and phone number of a therapist she heard is very good. I have seen him a few times. His name is Gordon. Last Thursday when I saw him I told him I wished the whole episode with Michael had never happened because it set me back and to do it was wrong. He asked, "Why wrong?" He thinks Michael was very important in my development because he validated my being me. I listened and tried on that idea and other related ones but I felt huge discomfort. Since then I've mulled the ideas over and today reached my conclusions which are different from Gordon's. I feel very strongly about my conclusions and think they will go a long way toward helping me resolve what has gone on.

First of all, what I did <u>was</u> wrong. I let myself get into a situation where I could fall in love with a married man and he could fall in love with me. I was tempted and I failed the test. I made a big mistake. I sinned. Now that all sounds very righteous, but in fact it was a moral issue and I blew it.

I remember specifically choosing to get to know Michael better in spite of the fact that he was married. I concluded in my mind that he didn't really have a marriage - and that was pure denial. I was tempted and I succumbed to the temptation by denying both reality and my morals.

It is also true that the giving and receiving of love I experienced with Michael was wonderful and beautiful and real. Loving like that is not wrong. It is one of God's greatest gifts - to love someone so much and be able to be loved so much in return. The loving experience wasn't wrong. The circumstances surrounding it were.

Contrary to what Gordon thinks, I didn't need Michael to open me up. I loved Dean very, very deeply for years. I have not had a problem loving deeply and well. What was new and wonderful for me with Michael was my feeling so completely loved by a man I adored - that was a truly rich experience. Yet, I wish I had not experienced it. The ecstatic man-woman love which I felt with Michael should be shared with someone who will be there for you forever, and you for him. The feelings felt true with Michael - but they were counterfeit due to his inability to appropriately commit to me. I was cheated. The experience felt right - but it was counterfeit. And the subsequent hurt for me was excruciating. Loving Michael served no good purpose for me in the end. Rather, it was exceedingly destructive to me. I would have been far better off to not have the love relationship with Michael. I didn't have a self-esteem problem for him to fix. I was well on my way to believing in myself and having the real me affirmed by myself and others before Michael came along.

September 24, 1993

Michael thinks his wife needs him more than I do. He seems to feel obligated to stay with her because she needs him, and not because she loves him more than I love him. I love Michael very, very much, and I want us to be together, but I won't be any man's mistress. And, if we don't end up together, I will survive somehow…and thrive again too.

Hmm…I wonder if Michael's therapist realized Michael's childhood relationships were codependent and that's what he wanted to work on with Michael? Sigh…

June 2, 1994

I am at the airport about to leave for the company's annual meeting. I can't say I'm excited about going and there are many valid reasons for that. In fact they are worth exploring because they tell a lot about who I am and where I am just now.

Michael will be at the meeting. How will I react when I see him? How do I want to react? I don't know the answer to either question. I do know that in the past I didn't want to control the strong attraction I had to him. Instead I dared to follow my fantasies and desires with him and his lack of trustworthiness broke me emotionally. I lowered my moral standards because the attraction was so strong and I was so needy for love.

Obviously I can't afford to jeopardize my new way of being by having any kind of personal encounter with Michael. I'm scared about my ability and resolve to pull this off. That man was like a bad drug for me. It was ecstasy when we fell in love and I became addicted to him and the situation. Then he didn't make good on his words to me and I went through severe withdrawal. I simply must not put myself in a situation with him in which he can pull me back in emotionally.

June 4, 1994

Michael attended the opening cocktail party on the first night of the company meeting. He came right over and spoke to me. I acknowledged him, but fortunately I was with others so I could turn back to them and continue the conversation. But I couldn't put on a front for very long. I went back to my hotel room within an hour and immediately broke down into uncontrollable sobbing which lasted a long time. At 2:00 a.m. I called the airlines and booked myself on a 6:00 a.m. flight back home. I chose to not stick it out at the meeting. The emotional pain was too great. I cried all the way to the airport and half of the way home on the flight. The closer I got to my own turf the better I felt. By leaving early I did what I needed to do to take care of myself.

August 11, 1994

I ran into Michael by chance a few weeks ago at a restaurant where I had joined others for a business lunch. Afterward, he left me a voicemail message thanking me for my smile and saying, "I would love to sit down and have lunch with you." I responded with a voicemail message telling him the pain of seeing him is so great for me I can't bear it. I told him I still believe at a gut level he and I should be together, but I understand we can't be and that conflict - plus the memories of what we had - trigger too much pain for me to get together with him. I begged him to not respond to my message.

September 24, 1994

God, tonight I want to pray as I write. I haven't prayed for a couple of days because I've had increasing doubt about the reality of faith. I am reading a book about the New Testament which is causing me to question what faith is. I've learned that in Moses' time people moved from polytheism to monotheism. And because 1200 years later people needed hope, they were ripe to believe in a redeemer. Do these understandings mean God and Jesus are like Santa and Mrs. Claus, mythical characters which inspire and give hope but are not real?

Oh my, I'm just too tired to continue this.

September 25, 1994

Reading about the sociology of the Greco-Roman Hellenistic period at the time of Jesus' life makes me think. At that time, honor was key. Unlike now when an individual's personal psychological introspection is valued, the Greco-Roman culture was based on group opinions. The family, and particularly the father, was responsible for the family's honor. There was a double standard sexually as well. The father could be sexually promiscuous without bringing shame, but the mother couldn't and preserve the family honor. The mother's honor was preserved by tending to the family. The father's honor was preserved by excelling outside the family and keeping his wife faithful. Isn't this the model Michael and his wife are practicing?

Also, this dedication to family honor is what my mother was all about. The family honor – the family image - was the most important thing in her life. And I supported her in this endeavor. The problem in my case was that the family image was saved at the expense of my individual development.

My mother died when she was fifty and I was fourteen. Three years after she died I brought shame to the family by getting sick with depression and needing to see a psychiatrist. My mother's sister, my favorite aunt, stopped being in contact with me when she heard I was seeing a psychiatrist. That was simply not an okay thing to do. In fact, it was shameful and a disgrace to my biological family.

Similarly for me, there has been a shamefulness attached to the act of getting divorced. Now I realize why. I was conditioned as a child to believe divorce was shameful - not just unfortunate. There is a difference.

And a key realization for me is that I got divorced because at some point I knew I needed to get out of a relationship in which I was not being honored. I came to know I needed to honor myself first, <u>before</u> my marital commitment. I concluded Dean would never honor me adequately. I chose my own personal honor above our family honor.

I believe right now that Michael is choosing family honor above his personal honor. He lives in a family value structure in which to be married and have an affair with me, or anyone else, still preserves his family's honor. But you know what? That arrangement doesn't support me. It's not good enough for me. What I have now is my personal honor. Having an affair with Michael satisfies his needs but not mine.

Also, I realize the guilt I have felt about hurting Michael's family is tied to my upbringing about family honor. I have felt guilt that my actions almost caused a situation to destroy <u>his</u> family's honor. OH MY! How much we are effected by our childhood conditioning.

October 2, 1994

<u>I am changing.</u> And this is significant change. I've been banged around enough now to link, maybe for the first time, my actions to what they

will mean to me - not just whether or not they will be morally good or bad. Something inside me tells me I am becoming an adult - not just responsible for whether or not I am good or bad (which a child can do). I now consider what the consequences of my actions may be for me and then I make an honest appraisal of whether or not I am willing to accept those consequences. How can I be fifty years old and just discovering this?! Somehow, I have lived all these years without considering what can hurt me. I've only considered whether or not something I am doing is morally right but not the real consequences to my life. Yikes!

October 10, 1994

Last week I attended a presentation on "Addictive Behavior" which was given at a nearby community hospital. The presentation was excellent and very relevant to my life experience. Based on what I heard, there is no doubt in my mind that I have been a "love addict" throughout my life. I learned the addiction in childhood, and I've been addicted three times – to my mother, to Dean, and to Michael.

Now I must change this behavior. I want to be free of love addiction and I believe I can be. After attending the class I finally know what has been wrong with me. I am a love addict (self-diagnosed) and my condition is curable. I just need to understand more about <u>what</u> is wrong and <u>why</u> it occurred. I need to do some exercises like the ones which were done in the class. I will read the suggested books and do the exercises in them.

October 19, 1994

My head is aching and my psyche is in extreme pain but I am doing the work I must do to heal my life - this I know at a gut level. Over the past three nights I have been reading a book I heard about at the Addictive Behavior presentation. The title of the book is *Facing Love Addiction*. The author is Pia Mellody. So far I have read to page 82.

How do I express the painful, slow healing that reading this book is bringing about? I am finally, finally, finally unlocking the terrible mysteries which have crippled me emotionally throughout my life. I don't have the energy just now to write down the many new awarenesses and realizations, but I need to write that they are happening. I am a "love addict" who is in withdrawal. I feel both hope and shock.

And I feel great pain. A lot of the pain is anger - intense anger at my mother who screwed me up royally. I'm realizing I experienced emotional abandonment as a child because my mother needed me to nurture her and I didn't get the nurturing I needed.

November 4, 1994

Things are changing for me. Gaining what I believe is truth in understanding about the codependent and love addiction patterns throughout my life, I am getting free. I am also viewing my faith from a reality versus fantasy perspective and this is setting me free. I'm not trusting anymore in the fantasy that God will provide for me on a minute to minute basis. I have to provide for myself. I have to make choices based on my thoughts and emotions and sense of values.

I no longer believe prayer works. By this I mean I don't think prayer really connects us to our creator. What I do believe is that prayer, as I have done it, let's me get in touch with myself by giving me a way to express my thoughts, feelings, needs, and gratitude...to think and feel aloud with myself...to review my spirit consciously at a particular point in time.

December 17, 1994

Michael left me a voicemail a week ago saying he had been to see Bernice's new baby. The message was full of apologies starting with "I know communication is verboten but..." and ending with "Sorry to have bothered you." I could feel his pain. I could feel how badly he wanted to be in touch with me. Rather than sending him a voicemail, I sent him a Christmas card.

When he got the card, he left me another very mixed up voicemail. First he thanked me for the card. Then he said he wanted to ask me something, "Would I be comfortable ever having a cup of coffee or lunch with him?" He said he wanted to engage in a direct conversation with me - that I was correct and he was wrong a while ago when I said I didn't think I could handle seeing him to talk to him. Then he referred to seeing me about a month ago (at a restaurant where I was with others from work) and having had a very difficult time handling it. That experience caused him to rethink his previous position and he didn't know how he would react to seeing me.

Prior to Michael's phone message, Bernice told me he came to see her and her new baby. She said he asked about me and ended up telling her he still loves me and always will. He said he had meant to leave his marriage or he wouldn't have told his kids about it. And he thought he was going to go to hell because of what he did to me.

After I listened to his voicemail I decided to leave him a voicemail response. My voicemail had two main points in it. First, I told him I had recently made a lot of progress detaching emotionally from him and I didn't want to chance going into a tail-spin. Secondly, I told him I have no negative feelings toward him - none at all - and that it is no longer a problem if I run into him. He needn't avoid running into me. I closed with "take care" and hung up.

January 13, 1995

Today Gordon and I talked about why I have suffered so much from Michael's abandonment of me. Gordon thinks it's directly related to the deep pain I experienced as a child when my mother abandoned me emotionally. He thinks the extent of that childhood abandonment justifies the time it is taking me to work through it, via Michael's abandonment of me. Now that I think about it, Michael's abandonment is like my mother's in another way. His words say one thing. His behavior says something else.

Gordon thinks the anger I have for my mother is important too. I <u>am</u> angry at her. What a crippling effect her life had on me. Gordon said that with a different mother my life could have been very different. But how can I blame someone who meant well but just didn't give me what I needed to get a good start in this world? I know she didn't do it on purpose. In fact, I believe she wanted very much to be a great mother. But the evidence is in - for who I am, she was not a great mother.

January 20, 1995

Today with Gordon I did more work with several pieces of my life's puzzle as I read from a book my mother wrote about her personal experience with cancer. The words showed her extreme need to control everything about her life, including her health. She also practiced – and taught my brother and me – to never think or say a negative thought. She firmly believed that what we think and say is what we create. However, my reality is now different from hers. I know having "negative" thoughts and feelings is part of being human. Repressing such thoughts and feelings ultimately makes a human being sick.

I told Gordon about the talk I had over Christmas with my mother's friend, Mara. When I went back home over the holidays to see my stepmother and her sister, I called Mara and asked if I could come to see her to talk about my mother. She said, "Of course, honey."

When I got to Mara's home I told her I wanted to learn from her about my mother. I mentioned my being only fourteen years old when my mother died and that there is a lot I don't know about her. The first thing Mara said about my mother was that she was a good cook. Then Mara noted that although she was a good friend of my mother, she experienced her as "very cold." She also told me she went to see my mother when she was in the hospital dying. During the visit my mother said she was sick because she had hate in her heart for Negroes and one of my brother's schoolmates. Mara and I didn't discuss the reference to Negroes, but Mara did tell me my mother said she hated my brother's schoolmate because he had beaten my brother out of something when they were competing in high school. Gordon noted that such a response embodied my mother's competitive instincts.

Mara also told me about an evening when my mother and father came to her house to play bridge. Because Mara knew I had participated in a music contest that day, she asked my mother how the contest went. My mother responded, "Susan got a #1 Rating and that's what we expected of her." Then Mara rolled her eyes at me, shrugged her shoulders, and sighed as she told me, "When she said that, I thought 'Oh dear.'"

Mara shared about a mutual friend of hers and my mother. The friend told her that my mother once asked why Mara was so nice to her (my mother). She also asked what Mara wanted from her. Mara was clearly hurt by the questions. These questions reminded me of Dean's regard for friends - they were for a self-serving purpose if they were for anything at all. UGH!

January 21, 1995

I am reading *The Christian Agnostic* by Leslie Weatherhead. This wonderful book is very relevant to my life right now. I just read the following passage:

> A statement is not true just because it is in the Bible, let alone in the Prayer Book...It has the AUTHORITY of the truth only when our own individual insight can leap up and recognize it and possess it as our own.

And in another place the author writes, "With what relief I mentally part with some of the views of Paul."

How important it is to me now to "mentally part with" many of the ways of my mother's life, of Dean's life, of Michael's life. What a relief it can be for me not to give my mother authority for the truth where her way of living is NOT right for me. And of course, the same is true related to Dean and Michael.

February 24, 1995

It is time for me to be brave, disciplined, and read my mother's manuscript which she didn't finish before she died. I feel strongly my reading of this document is a necessary hurdle for my psychological and spiritual development and my eventual well-being. I have had the document in my possession since Christmas but I have been unable to discipline myself to read it. I'm afraid of it because I don't want to be pulled back into the psychologically symbiotic relationship which I had with my mother when I was a child. I also fear I will like her or agree with her, and I am just recently identifying and validating how she and her behavior hurt me. Recognizing these hurts and their causes is helping me now. If I like her in this manuscript, I may become confused again. But...I know I must do this.

Later - Well, I just read the preface and the first two chapters of my mother's unfinished manuscript for a book she was planning to title *Beyond Religion*. There is no doubt about it, my mother was brilliant. Not only was she brilliant, her portrayal of herself is truly one of sainthood.

The presentation of her beliefs is authoritative and without question in her mind. The only possible crack in her armor - in my opinion - is her insistence that she has the power of God at her disposal if she is tenacious and skilled enough at connecting to it. For me, there is a sincere humbleness missing. I am also feeling overwhelmed by the responsibility she requires of herself and others to practice and learn to connect with God and God's power through breathing exercises, meditations, and affirmations. She believes these practices enable human beings to cure themselves from illness, maintain excellent health, protect themselves in every way, and accomplish whatever they want to accomplish in their lives.

Later Still - I have just completed the third chapter. It is, for the most part, as I remember things. I do find my mother's use of quotations from my brother and me to be a bit rigged and <u>very</u> self-serving. She quotes us with words which are quite unlikely to come out of the mouths of real children and these words are clearly designed to highlight her prowess at being a wise and effective mother. I also noted an emerging imperative that an individual must be in total control of his/her life.

February 27, 1995

I just finished reading Chapter 9 of my mother's manuscript.

My mother was a genius - there is no doubt about it. She was also, and perhaps because she was a genius, so far out of the mainstream in her thinking that I am dizzy reading her stuff. I wonder if my therapist or minister would think she was a little crazy if they read her stuff. I think she was definitely crazy. No wonder I am suffering the pangs of emotional abandonment. I don't think she was capable of being a normal mother. Her mind and her sense of who she was - an elite and spiritually superior personality - would probably have prevented her from being a normal mother. She was definitely <u>not</u> a normal person.

April 6, 1995

This afternoon I met with my minister for almost two hours. In preparation for our meeting I had given him three things: (1) a copy of an article my mother wrote about her demanding Caesarian births to deliver my brother and me – in order to not ruin her sex life by having vaginal births (2) a copy of the Introduction to her unpublished manuscript, and (3) the first chapter of the same manuscript. When I arrived, I showed my minister a photo of my mother and told him a little about her. Then we talked about her writings.

While exploring the article my mother wrote about demanding Cesarean births, I found it obvious my mother participated in life in a somewhat detached manner. She seemed to have prepared for and delivered two babies almost as much as an observer as a participant. It was obvious her first priority was to be in control and not overwhelmed. The births were a performance for her to impress herself and others with her strength and ability to handle everything without getting ruffled. Her only comment about my brother was that he was perfect. And the only instance of expressed anxiety came from my father who asked if there was something wrong with me when I was born blue (which was a result of my not having started to breathe yet). My mother's reaction to my being blue was not a concern for her new baby but her fear that I might not be perfect. I suspect she simply couldn't stand to have anything associated with her be less than perfect!

In the Introduction of her manuscript, my mother flips from talking about how she is writing the book for "you" (my brother and me) to a much more generic "you" as the writing goes on. The message doesn't maintain the intimacy which the first sentence suggests. Instead she seems to take on a detached mode of a philosopher or sociologist. My minister noted this without my prompting him. I had written in the margin of my copy, "I don't believe she really wrote this for us. I think she wrote it for herself and her own glorification." Then the idea flickered in my mind of narcissism. She was most definitely narcissistic. Indeed the whole manuscript smacks of it.

Next my minister commented on another paragraph which I had highlighted. He thought it was noteworthy that she said, "...youth are apt to be so healthy, vigorous, busy and happy that they may neglect to remember and practice consistently that which they have been taught." He found it strange that being healthy, vigorous, and happy wasn't enough.

The next two sentences were significant to me. My mother suggests she is writing this book to capture the techniques my brother and I will need when we're lost and groping because we've neglected to practice what she taught us. Give me a break! In other words, when we are having trouble it will be our fault because we didn't follow her design. Of course her design for living couldn't be faulty could it? It would have to be our failure to practice it well!

As we continued to look at the manuscript, I reflected on one of my minister's earlier comments - that in the first chapter he saw no new ideas from what was prevalent at the time. I began to remember another realization I experienced toward the end of my relationship with Dean and throughout the entire divorce process. With Dean, I went from regarding him as incredibly smart and knowledgeable, to seeing him as arrogant and not really smart. He had me fooled that he was very, very bright right up until the end of our marriage when I began to know he was a lot of boastful self-confidence which was more than a bit unfounded. The same kind of awakening began to occur in me regarding my mother as I processed my mother's manuscript with my minister.

And last but by no means least, as my minister pointed out my mother's detachedness, it suddenly seemed to me that a synonym for detachment could be emotional abandonment. And what was the basic thesis presented by Pia Mellody for the cause of love addiction? Yes, abandonment - physical or emotional abandonment. My narcissistic, arrogant mother spoke of dedicating her book to her children. The reality is, she verbally abandons that intimacy even on the first page of the Introduction. How much did she play this observer/abandoner role in her day-to-day relationship with me? I suspect a lot. Why else would I have put up with it for so long with Dean? It was what I knew.

Similarly, an extension of my thoughts about abandonment came to me in church last Sunday when we read the scripture passage in which Judas approaches Jesus with a kiss and then betrays him. Isn't that what my mother did? The kiss was the "To My Children" lead-in for her manuscript. The betrayal/abandonment follows. And who else approached me with a kiss and then betrayed/abandoned me? Yes, of course, Michael. Actually he is the one I thought of when we read the Judas story. He, like Judas, wasn't strong enough to take the heat and stay true to his heart. Perhaps that analogy is a stretch but the abandonment of my mother, and Dean, and Michael were real. And all that I needed in each of these three relationships was a genuine love for me, a love which wasn't counterfeit. But none of these people delivered that. Perhaps they were not capable of it.

April 18, 1995

Tonight on TV a Jewish woman rabbi talked about Passover. She explained Passover is a celebration of freedom. Then she said freedom has two parts to it. One part is the part which involves being released from bondage and the other part is the part which involves reaching toward a new existence. As I ponder these ideas, I realize I'm not putting enough emphasis on reaching toward my new existence. I will soon complete the work I need to do to understand my bondages of the past (codependency and love addiction with my mother, Dean, and Michael), but I have not worked anywhere near as hard at envisioning the future I want, identifying the goals to make the vision happen, and then developing the action plans to realize the goals and vision. I suspect doing this work will be very uplifting for me.

May 6, 1995

My brain is telling me I should be writing. I've just been sobbing for about ten minutes. I've felt sad this afternoon and then while reading an article about a mother, her child, and her child's friend who was given love by the mother, I started to cry. And I suddenly felt like I was a little girl again. I could even imagine the French braids I had when I was little. And I felt so needy for love. So needy for someone to <u>really</u> love me. For someone to really love <u>me</u>. And even now I'm sobbing again. I so want to be loved. I so want someone to hold me and let me feel a love which surrounds me and protects me and makes me know I am truly wonderful. Oh Mother, please come and love me, really love me. That's what I need. That's what I'm searching for. Where are you? Why don't you come to me? I feel so alone. So alone and so needy. I don't know why you won't come. I need you. My heart is breaking. I feel so alone. I need to be loved...

And I just remembered I was put in an incubator when I was born because I was born six weeks early. I wonder if I felt alone then?

And I am remembering the evening after the afternoon my mother died. My school friends came to the house and one of them asked me to play Bumble Boogie on the piano. I did it. How bizarre. My mother had just died and I didn't, or couldn't, acknowledge it. What strange behavior I exhibited. As I think about it now, I guess I didn't know how to be sad with others. I didn't have a clue about how to be real then. How strange and unfortunate.

I remember the horrible feelings of homesickness I experienced three times in my elementary school years - when I was invited to spend the night at two friends' homes and at a 5-day overnight summer camp. In all three instances I cried and cried until my mother was called to come pick me up and take me home.

And then in my freshman year of college, the feelings of depression became unbearable, and Dad and Betty came. And soon thereafter I started psychotherapy.

As I sit here right now, I realize I'm fifty years old and I want to be mothered. I don't necessarily want _my_ mother, but I want to be mothered. I want someone to just love me because I'm hurting – not to ask why I'm hurting or tell me how to stop hurting, but to just hold me and love me and let the hurt go away on its own.

Oh my, now I am realizing the experience I had with Michael in the beginning is what I've longed for since birth. Michael held me. Michael kissed me. Michael told me I was wonderful. I was so happy. And then the impossible began to happen. The love I had found - after so much pain - became jeopardized. My heart and soul were traumatized again, almost unbearably.

And now many months later, a protective, defensive reaction is occurring in me. I am criticizing Michael. I am criticizing my mother. It feels better than the hurt, but it also feels bad - bad because it is judgmental. And I don't like to "do" judgment...or...am I doing discernment of reality rather than judgment of others? Hmm...

June 3, 1995
New thoughts of personal empowerment to catapult me over and beyond Michael:

— I no longer want or need what the relationship with Michael provided.
— My shame about the relationship is gone because I now view it as a learning experience which taught me volumes about myself, my past relationships, and my vulnerabilities.
— By choosing not to care what Michael thinks of me, I will give myself the power to protect myself from him.

The three preceding affirmations will be my armor at the upcoming annual company meeting. By repeating them and asking for God's help, I believe I will be fine at the meeting. I am not afraid to go now. I will be safe whether Michael is there or not. If he is there, I will avoid him. If he ends up in a group with me, I will say "hi" to him if the situation requires it and then I will focus on whatever the group is working on.

June 5, 1995
I just got home from the annual company meeting.

I feel strong. I feel grateful. I feel only a little, tiny bit tentative now about moving on. I am detaching at long last from Michael - an angel and a devil in my life.

I saw him. I played golf with him and five others. And all the time I was relaxed, calm, and able to maintain healthy boundaries. I didn't flirt. I wasn't rude. I was appropriately friendly and fun on the golf course and I was appropriately inattentive at meals and meetings.

Michael is a weak, lost soul, and I wish him well – although I believe his patterns of weak behavior are very well-established. I was told some months ago he is having an affair with a work colleague. On the golf course I thought I saw the evidence. She was one of the six of us who played together. How bizarre...Michael, this woman, me, and three other men all playing golf together. How strange that must have felt to Michael. Or perhaps he loved it - two trophies side by side! YUCK!!! How totally disgusting!!

Yet I find I don't care tonight. Oh I care I was in such a ridiculous and embarrassing situation as to be playing golf with a married man whom I have loved and who is now the other woman's lover. But I really don't care if he's having an affair with her. Let them make love all they want. I quite amazingly and wonderfully don't care anymore.

What a wonderful feeling! I don't care! I just <u>don't</u> care!!! It <u>is</u> over. I'm moving on and I'm so grateful it is over and I'm moving on. Thanks be to You, God!

June 17, 1995
I think I would like to take a course at a seminary. I want to learn what ministers know. When I listen to my minister's wonderful sermons or meet with him for pastoral care, I am very aware his knowledge of human life includes perspectives unknown to me.

My authentic self is consistently drawn to spiritual things. This was true many years ago in my late adolescent and early adult years. And the attraction and feelings nipped at me during the years of my marriage with Dean - but I had to push them down and away then because they were unappreciated and unsupported in my life with him. Now I can choose to address my interest and my sense of attraction to spiritual things.

I need to find seminaries which are close to where I live or work. Then I need to request their catalogs to find pastoral care courses which interest me and are held on weekday evenings. I want to take one course at a time while continuing to work full-time in the corporate business world.

September 7, 1995

This evening I will attend my first class at seminary. Yea! I decided to make my first course a systematic theology course. That means the course content will systematically explore Christian theories on specific topics. For this term the topics are Humanity, Christology, and God. I am eager to learn about historical and contemporary Christian thinking on these topics. For future terms, I will choose pastoral care courses in order to increase my understanding regarding the psychological and spiritual nature of human beings.

I am very excited to be going to my first class at seminary.

September 22, 1995

Last night was the third class in the theology course I am taking. The class is wonderful. I am absolutely entranced with the material. I'm spending hours and hours reading the many assignments. No skimming for me. I'm too interested. I keep a dictionary by my side. All of the new terms are a bit overwhelming but I am starting to recognize and understand them.

The professor is excellent. He is articulate, faith full, competent as a theologian and teacher, and a very nice, sensitive person. He is also very comfortable with who he is, and he is sincerely concerned about giving to his students. The time flies by quickly in the classes and I wish they lasted longer! I really couldn't be any more interested in the readings. I'm so glad I kept my schedule free to study evenings and week-ends. So far, I am loving seminary.

The first assignment was for students to write a one-page reflection on their personal theology. I wrote candidly. The professor handed back the reflections last night and wrote on my paper, "Thank you for this wonderfully clear and open statement. Great start." I am very pleased with his response.

October 28, 1995

I am feeling better about myself and my life, and I am grateful for the improvement. That is not to say I am completely "out of the woods" regarding Michael and other historical traumas. But I have definitely moved on, and I believe my understanding of my life and myself is significantly improved.

Now I am going to write something shocking. Last night I figured out I hate my mother. I hate who she was and I hate what she did to me. I think she was an arrogant, self-serving, highly narcissistic woman who lacked compassion and didn't come close to meeting my psycho-spiritual needs as an infant or child. Because of her I have had many losses in my life which didn't need to be.

I recognized and wrote down similar thoughts last night as I listened to John Bradshaw's tape "Home Coming." A friend thought I might enjoy the tape. The experience of going back to my infancy and toddlerhood was very rich. I'm too tired to write more about it all tonight, but it brought me to a place where I can say I hate "her" (my mother) with hardly any guilt and - wonderfully - without fear! How strangely freeing these thoughts and words are for me. I hate who she was and what she did to me, and I am particularly angry she indoctrinated me in the destructive beliefs of the religious cult she embraced. How dare she take a young, impressionable child and fill her up with such misguided, destructive doctrine. I am enraged about that!

This religious part of my upbringing has become much more poignant to me since I started the theology course. Studying different theologians' perspectives on "humanity" (the human condition) helped me become aware of new ways to think and to dare to write down my own thoughts on the topic. In many ways my own thoughts reflected my relationship with my mother, as well as imprints in me from the doctrines of the religious cult in which my mother believed. Very scary to discover!

November 15, 1995
One of the options for the next paper in theology class is to write my personal views on "Christology" (my beliefs about Jesus) in a letter. I started a letter for the class but the exercise developed a life of its own as I realized I needed to write a letter to my deceased mother <u>before</u> I wrote the assignment for the class.

What an incredible experience it was to write to my mother! The letter is an analysis of my life and the many destructive effects I believe my mother had on me. It is also an account of the considerable anger I have for my mother. And, it is a sacred letter – sacred because writing it helped me become more in touch with my own psycho-spiritual journey. The letter follows:

> Dear Mother,
> I am fifty-one years old now - a year older than you were when you died. The good news is my mid-life years are bringing me God's saving grace and understanding. The bad news is my life - until recently - has been filled with intense psycho-spiritual pain caused to a large degree by you and your theology.
>
> You taught me I am God in human form and therefore I can make myself free of disease, free from harm, and able to excel in all my endeavors if I conscientiously practice the breathing

exercises, meditations, and affirmations of the religious cult you embraced.

I was three years old when you were diagnosed with breast cancer and treated with a mastectomy as well as 100+ x-ray treatments. Shortly after the surgery and x-ray treatments you responded to a flyer in the mail sent by a religious cult located far away. You wrote to the cult's leader to receive materials and immediately began practicing the cult's teachings. You embraced these teachings without reservation and came to believe you healed yourself of the cancer by using the techniques of the cult. You even took our family of four to the site of the cult to attend conventions in which we learned the cult's teachings and techniques. I was 8, 10, and 12 years old when I attended those conventions.

Ten years after your diagnosis with breast cancer, lung cancer appeared in your body. On your death bed about six months later, you told me you could have healed yourself again but you were just too tired to do it. After you died I continued to grieve your death and faithfully practice the teachings and techniques of the cult for many years.

Mother, you taught me Jesus was a great man - but a man who was no more divine than any other. You said he didn't really die on the cross; rather, he was taken to the tomb still alive and he used techniques similar to those of the religious cult to heal himself in the tomb. You also said Jesus was so highly skilled in using those techniques he could make himself appear to the disciples without really being with them in a physical body. You told me Jesus probably went away to a mountain top somewhere and lived out the rest of his life after the seeming resurrection. And even with all of this rejection of the fundamentals of Christianity, you had our family attend a Christian church near our home and then arranged to have the minister of that church officiate at your funeral.

For the fourteen years I knew you Mother, you were so confident in yourself, so arrogant, and so in control of yourself and others, I learned to worship you like a god. I became your disciple, living for you as the perfect daughter in order to glorify you. My sole identity and mission in life was being your perfect daughter.

You taught me our family was supposed to be different from - and better than - other families. You taught me to keep things within the family and not to discuss family things with others. A neighbor once told me no one on our street ever knew what was going on in our house.

Not surprisingly, I married a man who was very much like you, Mother. He was confident, arrogant, industrious, controlling, closed, manipulative of others, and - in the end - vengeful. For many years I was the perfect wife, living for him and trying to satisfy his every wish - including his wish to not have children because he didn't want to "invest the time and money children would require." I left him four years ago after twenty years of marriage. As I finally began to become my own person in my mid-forties, I found I could no longer deny how unacceptable his behaviors and values were to me. For several years I asked him to go to a marriage counselor with me but he refused. So I went alone - off and on - over four years. Finally I filed for a divorce and left him.

A few months after leaving my husband, I felt wonderfully relieved, peaceful, and extraordinarily loved by God. You see, I had gone to a neighborhood church in my distress and my needs were met there. The sermons, the prayers, the people, and the teachings of Jesus validated my despair. I was accepted, cared for, and loved, even though I was weak and very needy. I instantly felt "at home" in the church and was very grateful for my new church family. One morning as I prayed, I asked myself and God what I should do with my new life – in order that at the end of the next ten years I would be proud of how I had invested my time. The idea came into my head that I could attend a seminary to learn what ministers know. The thought caused me to feel happy and hopeful.

But just six months later a horrible period in my life ensued. I was assigned to a project with a handsome, articulate, business man who, on the first day we worked together, asked me about my aspirations in the company. I told him I didn't know what my aspirations were because I was going through a big transition in my life. He asked what the transition was and I told him it was a divorce. Then he told me he had been unhappy in his marriage for the preceding fifteen years of his almost thirty-year marriage. In only a few weeks I was hopelessly in love with this man who said to me all the words of love and caring which I had needed to hear my entire life. He told me he loved me and wanted me to be his life partner. He told his wife he was in love with me and then with her agreement sold their house and started looking for apartments for both of them. I was absolutely intoxicated with love and believed God had given us to each other as a very special gift.

But the inconceivable followed. After several months, the man's wife fell apart emotionally and he was consumed with guilt. He began saying he wasn't sure he could leave her and he had learned from my divorce story that he hadn't tried hard enough to make his marriage work. I was shocked, devastated, and torn with guilt. I told him he should try to make his marriage work if he could - hoping all the while he would discover he couldn't live without me, based on the things he had said to me and the intoxicating joy we had known.

Over the next two years this man continued to periodically call me and tell me he missed me and was still in love with me. That period and the following year were the darkest of my life. As the months went by, my addictive attachment to him broke me emotionally. I stayed away from him physically, but the withdrawal and guilt I suffered were unparalleled pain for me. My friends, my minister, and my therapist continued to support me through the many phases of my brokenness: the agonizing grief, the horrible guilt, the feelings of estrangement from God, the feelings of disillusionment with God, the experience of repentance, and finally the gift of once more feeling God's love, forgiveness, and grace in my life.

Mother, I am very angry at you. I believe you are the root cause of most of the anguish I have just described. I hate who you were and I hate what you did to me. Your egotism, power, and controlling nature robbed me of my right and need to develop my own identity. Your indoctrination of me with the religious cult's ideology brainwashed me with a theology which was unrealistic and destructive. You and your theology didn't teach me that failure, brokenness, pain, and sin are mortal and necessary experiences. You didn't teach me love can exist without requiring performance. You didn't teach me God is God, and I am God's beloved child. You didn't teach me God's grace is a gift which cannot be controlled. You didn't teach me I need to openly embrace others in community in order that I may both give and receive support in a loving, healthy way.

Mother, I am not afraid of you or your power over me anymore. I am very angry at you, but in time I believe the anger will be replaced with compassion for the confused, fearful soul you were.

And despite my current anger at you, I am nonetheless very grateful and hopeful. I am grateful for God's grace which is leading me through enlightenment about my propensity for addictive relationships. I am grateful for my friends and minister and therapists who have loved me and cared for me through all of my brokenness. I am grateful for my new identity as God's beloved child, a child who is loved simply because I am and not for how I look or how well I perform. I am grateful for my faith and church community which support and nurture my considerable spiritual needs. And I have hope that soon the emotional and spiritual wounds of the past will heal over and in their place will be scars that are ever so much stronger than the original materials. Then, with God's continued grace, I believe I will find a way to laugh and love and serve in a wonderfully Christian way for the rest of my life.

Your daughter,
Susan

December 28, 1995

For the second day in a row, I have worked in the training room at the office location where Michael works. Yesterday as I was leading a full-day workshop, he circled around the glass walls of the training room two or three times. It was easy to ignore him then because I was focused on leading the workshop. (I was startled the first time he came around, but I was able to recover quickly and go on comfortably and effectively.) There was absolutely no reason for him to come over to the training room side of the building except to see me. I did not acknowledge him, which was not obviously rude because he was always a good distance away from me. And each time he came into view I was leading the group or talking with a participant.

I didn't feel too affected by it all when I got home last night, but I woke up at 2:45 AM this morning and couldn't go back to sleep.

Then today, I suspect someone told Michael I was there again. About noon he came to the training room and poked his head in. I was busy documenting the previous day's workshop results on a computer in the back of the room. A group of five other people who know Michael was meeting in the front of the room. As he appeared in the doorway, everyone turned to speak to him. He spoke to them and greeted me. I responded and listened to the banter between him and the group for a couple minutes and then resumed typing. He chatted with the group for about fifteen minutes and twice turned to me and asked a question. Both times I had to ask him to repeat the question because I was typing and not listening. Each time I went right back to my computer work. He finally left the room without turning to acknowledge me again.

I felt and feel angry at him. If he really cared about me - before or now - he would have stayed away. But I know him. He wanted to see me and he wanted me to see him and get all excited again. It didn't work. And quite frankly it disgusted me that he's either so selfish and/or so conceited he had to make his presence known to me.

January 10, 1996
Today I sat at a desk in the "stacks" of the seminary's library reading a book for the course I am taking during this winter term about healing bridges between religion and medicine. The book is *Healing Body and Soul* by John A. Sanford. As I read the author's description of Carl Jung's concept of "individuation," my attention became more and more intense. Then I had a major moment of illumination. I looked up, quietly laid the book down on the desk, and thought to myself, "Individuation is why I am here in seminary. Individuation is what I have been working on for several years." After that I stood up and slowly walked amid the stacks of books for quite a while, taking in my new awareness. I concluded there is a name and a purpose for the journey I am on…the journey of individuation!

January 11, 1996
I now realize I was first introduced to the idea of individuation several years ago when the marriage counselor I was seeing mentioned something about figuring out "who you are supposed to be." The phrase caught my attention and caused me to consider whether or not there is

a predetermined profile of who each person is meant to become. John Sanford's book clarifies this perspective – a perspective of hope for me – that there is within each human being a wisdom and longing to guide each of us into our own unique wholeness. Our job is to find out what our unique profile is and actualize it.

This thinking is very important to me personally because it is counter to the destructive psychological environment in which I grew up. As the daughter of a powerful, famous, terminally ill mother, I grew up trying to be the perfect daughter. I put all of my energy into being exactly what she wanted me to be. I didn't develop the "me" of me. I had no identity beyond being my mother's daughter. Then as a young adult I repeated the behavior by falling in love with a powerful man with whom I prioritized being the perfect wife. So until mid-life, I was an unknowing victim of others' egocentricities.

Jung and Sanford's ideas suggest to me that true individuation mitigates against the egocentricities of those who try to control others. It also mitigates against the dysfunction of codependency for those of us who were taught to be egoless in order to unconditionally support the other powerful people in our lives. I believe the concept of individuation is powerful in a life-enhancing way, and I am very grateful to have learned about it.

February 5, 1996
Today the spring term began. After feeling excited about taking a course on pastoral approaches to illness and dying, I had two upsetting experiences at the beginning of the class. One of the professors (the class is being team-taught) asked the students to do a meditation centered on someone who had come to see us when we were down and who made us feel uplifted and at peace. I couldn't immediately recall such a person or experience and that made me sad, uncomfortable, and tense. Then I realized my

profound experiences of being uplifted and at peace have happened when I am by myself praying, or writing in my diaries, or crying to express the deep hurts and losses - or rich joys and gratitude - which I have known. During those times I have known a sense of inner wisdom and love. So I remembered those times and yet I felt inadequate because I couldn't follow the directions given by the professor.

Next the professor asked us to become aware of our breath. Unfortunately that directive was a negative trigger for me. I flashed back to the hours and hours I sat in meditation at the training conventions of the religious cult my mother embraced. Those meditations were meaningless to me even though I tried my best to do what I was told. I suspect I was just too young for meditation. I was only 8, 10, and 12 years old.

And now I'm angry. I'm angry yet again at my mother. Her indoctrination of me in that cult has caused me a lifetime of confusion. She was so damn egocentric I'm sure she never even gave thought to whether or not the exposure would be good for the rest of the family. She wanted to do it and she just dragged the whole family through it. That is the way the family was. Whatever my mother wanted, we all did. My father didn't buy the cult's philosophy, but he was so meek and mild he would never have questioned my mother's wishes. Would that Daddy had distinguished himself by letting her do it, but not feeling obligated to do it himself - and not letting her indoctrinate my brother and me. I think it is significant that after my mother died, my father returned to his own faith and became a very happy Christian man with a wonderful Christian wife. In fact, I saw Betty love my father into his own true identity – a magnificent transformation to behold!

So, I've learned over the years I have to do the work of remembering what things were like a long time ago, experience the discomfort again, recognize the losses which have ensued, and then evaluate the experiences as an adult. Some of my adult conclusions are:

— I was uncomfortable meditating as a child because I didn't feel any-thing significant and I knew I was supposed to.

— I was indoctrinated as a child in the teachings of the religious cult my mother embraced and I am still working out life-depleting ele-ments of that indoctrination. Today in class, experiencing a medi-tation exercise triggered past memories of meditation which are upsetting to me.

— This triggering mechanism may mean I will require some special adjustments to the meditation exercises in class - until I can work through the triggers. Perhaps I can have an understanding with the instructors that if I become uncomfortable, I can open my eyes and stretch quietly – not out of disrespect but out of the situational handicap I'm experiencing.

— I don't want to leave the class and I do believe meditation can be wonderfully therapeutic for people. I just need to be where I am right now and not reach the conclusion I will always be uncomfort-able with meditation just because I had a terrible childhood experi-ence surrounding the practice.

March 25, 1996

The first written assignment for the pastoral approaches course was due last week. Each student was asked to write a reflection paper regarding who s/he is. I wrote from my heart about my background and my reasons for coming to seminary. I also wrote about how difficult some of the class activities are for me and why.

I was pleased to finally feel understood and supported by the professor who read my paper. She wrote on it, "Susan, I am grateful you shared so directly from your heart in this paper. I now more deeply appreciate the dimensions of the challenges you face each week in class! I am awed by your courage and willingness to revisit these traumatic memories in order to truly put them in the past. Please continue to stay in touch and let me know any ways I can further your healing. I support you amending <u>any</u> instructions or suggestions to better fit your needs."

July 17, 1996

For the addiction class I am taking this summer, students have been required to write a reflection paper each week on assigned readings. Last week we were asked to write a reflection on a book about addiction which we had personally selected. I chose Pia Mellody's book, *Facing Love Addiction* - a book I first read a couple of years ago. The experience of writing a paper on this book at this point in my life was extremely valuable to me.

I want to record two of the sections I put in my reflection paper:

<u>Love Addiction Symptoms I Have Experienced</u>
— Difficulty setting functional boundaries with my partner
— Difficulty owning my reality appropriately - knowing who I am and how to share that
— Difficulty facing the realities of who my partner is and what is going on
— Difficulty having a healthy relationship with myself
— Difficulty sharing my own reality
— Allowing my partner to dictate who I should be in order to keep him/her comfortable
— Making my partner my Higher Power
— Assigning a disproportionate amount of time, attention, and "value above myself" to my partner - a focus with an obsessive quality to it
— Neglecting to care for or value myself when in a relationship

<u>Causes of Love Addiction I Have Experienced</u>
— Because my mother abandoned me emotionally in my early life, I repressed unhealed pain.

— Because I was not nurtured for who I was as a child, I did not learn how to be my natural self.
— Because my natural characteristics were not nurtured, I developed dysfunctional coping behaviors and did not learn good self-nurturing skills.
— Because I did not learn how to have a healthy relationship with myself, I turned to "being in love" to fill the emptiness and hide the pain.
— Because I was both emotionally needy and used to supplying unconditional devotion to my powerful mother, I was attracted to powerful people who gushed over me and responded to my adoration for them.
— Because I had experienced emotional abandonment as a child, I was attracted to people who were incapable of real intimacy.
— Although being in love with the people I chose was an emotional roller coaster, I denied the "lows" because the "highs" felt so good. I became addicted to the "highs."
— Only when I began to truly value myself did I begin to see that the emotional roller coaster ride with my highly narcissistic husband wasn't good enough for me.

August 14, 1996

Last week's reading and reflection assignment for the addiction class was the book *Taking On The Gods* by Merle Jordan. This short but amazing book is jam-packed with wisdom – including explanations for most of the major dysfunctions in my life. Incredible! Tonight I want to write about a new awareness which came to me after I turned in my reflection paper.

Jordan writes about the cross the pastoral counselor bears when a client chooses not to change - thereby resisting God's grace and the Good News. He also speaks of the "secular idols" a client may choose to continue to hold on to – values or beliefs the client feels more comfortable holding on to rather than taking the risk to turn to God and let go of the old values and beliefs.

All of this made me think of Michael and the deep pain I felt when he decided to stay in his home situation. Not only was I deeply distraught at losing him as the man I loved; I was also deeply distraught because he chose to turn back to his family's values and beliefs, saying "no" to God's grace. I loved Michael's very soul and I believed the love we felt for each other was a gift from God. But Michael wasn't able to choose a new life for himself, and me, and us. He chose instead to hold on to the familiar life he had known.

Also, today in class when we discussed Tillich's ideas on destiny, I better understood the battle Michael faced. Tillich described destiny as the sum total of a person's DNA - including family, education, values, decisions, etc. He believed all of the elements of who someone is effect and become the person's destiny. Destiny is, therefore, like character. And I realized Michael was fighting to change himself from a lifetime of character elements which were so deeply entrenched in him, he was only able to choose minor changes for his life, rather than major ones. Oh my, how I grieved his choice. But it was <u>his</u> choice to make. I loved him and I lost him. But so did God, and I grieve for God too.

December 13, 1996
I took a class on Christian personal ethics this term. Having previously made the shameful choice to fall in love with a married man, I thought I sorely needed a course in ethics! Much to my amazement the course helped me considerably to understand why I made the choices I made with both Dean and Michael, and why Michael ultimately decided to stay in his marriage. I now think I stayed with Dean for such a long time based on "rules-based" ethics - what I perceived to be the dutiful, right thing to do. And then as Dean's behavior grew to be more and more offensive to me, I moved on to "the ends justify the means" ethics - believing I needed to leave Dean

in order to achieve my own human flourishing. And when I met Michael and he said he had been unhappy in his marriage for the fifteen preceding years, I believed he was at a point of choosing to leave his wife from "the ends justify the means" ethics - in order for him to flourish and become who he was designed to be. But in the end, his upbringing in "rules-based" ethics caused him to return to his dutiful choice of fulfilling the letter of the marriage law, rather than the authentic substance of his heart and soul.

The ethics class also helped me understand how to interpret situations in the business world from a Christian base. I explored that learning in my final term paper, an ethical argument I wrote titled "The Business World: Its Demons and Its Hope." In that paper I was able to document my ethical concerns and frustrations with the business world and then address the concerns and frustrations from a Christian base. I worked very hard on the paper and forced myself to grapple with many new ideas.

I find I am now interested in seeing how I will be different in the business world going forward. I know I have changed during this school term. I am much stronger in my Christian identity. I think it is very likely I will be compelled to gently bring some Christian-based ethics into the business world. I wonder how my colleagues will react to that. And because I now understand a person's ethics are his/her character and destiny, I wonder how my destiny in the business world will play out in view of my changed identity. I suspect I will have more compassion for my work colleagues, remembering an individual's ethical views were instilled by the person's family and societal culture. Perhaps I will also feel more confident to suggest life-enhancing ways to frame, understand, and address specific incidents for the good of all involved.

January 16, 1997

I need to write a paper for the bereavement class I am taking during this winter term. The assignment is for each student to write about a loss and grief s/he has experienced. I have decided to write about my father's death which occurred almost eight years ago. And I want to write about it first in this diary, remembering him with love. Here goes…

My father died two weeks short of his eighty-third birthday. He died on a doctor's examination table far away from home, where he and my stepmother, Betty, were visiting with her family. He died of a massive coronary.

At the same time my father was dying, I picked up the phone in my office at work and called his home to see if he and Betty had, in fact, left on their trip as scheduled. Something made me want to check up on him. When no one answered the phone I assumed they had left as planned a few days before. Two hours later my brother called my manager at work with the news our father had died.

When my manager spoke with me I immediately knew I must go to Betty, see Daddy, arrange for his cremation (which he had previously requested), drive Betty back home in their car, and set up a memorial service in their hometown. When I called my brother he said he didn't need to see our father again. He didn't want to make the trip - even though he lived much closer than I did to where our father died. I felt very differently. I knew I wanted to see Daddy one last time.

The next day on the jet I cried the entire trip to Betty's family home. My husband didn't want to go and I went alone. It was as if my tear ducts had a limitless supply of tears which rolled down my checks hour after hour. I sensed Daddy's presence throughout the trip. When I got to the town where he was to be cremated, I went to find Betty. Understandably, she was in a state of shock and I felt very responsible for her. She suggested I go in to see Daddy alone as she had already seen him. I entered the room feeling tense and reverent. I was overwhelmed with emotion when I saw him.

I touched his hand and cried, and cried, and prayed, and talked to him, and cried some more. He looked almost as though he was alive and I felt enormous love for him, and loss, and sadness. I was very glad I had come. Finally, I knew it was time for me to leave him. That was one of the hardest things I have ever done.

I drove Betty home. During those three days, I tried my best to give her silent time to grieve, as well as time for conversation when she wanted to talk. I totally followed her lead. The nights with her in the motel rooms felt strange. She had trouble sleeping and was very confused.

When we got back to her home I made all of the plans for the memorial service. I visited the minister whom I knew a little bit and I cried and cried in his presence. Then I went off to the chapel to write my part of the service and I cried and cried some more. Surprisingly, writing down my thoughts for the service was very cathartic and deeply meaningful for me.

At the memorial service, family and friends were not afraid to talk about Daddy. And over the years since his death I have made it a point to talk about him as the spirit inspires me to do so. Around Betty, who now suffers from senile dementia, I try to be a good listener and provide her the opportunity to tell her stories over and over about their wonderful marriage. She suffered an enormous loss when Daddy died, and then a few years later she suffered another when it was time to sell their home (of twenty-six years) and move into a retirement community. I helped her move and felt both compassion and frustration as she tried to accept the change amid her sadness and the increasing symptoms of her dementia. She still misses my father mightily and always will. Their marriage was the most wonderful marriage I have ever seen.

I feel blessed with the bereavement process I have gone through for my father. I was able to significantly participate in the event of his death by going to see him, taking responsibility for Betty, and planning and participating in his memorial service. Later on I arranged for a cemetery stone and was present at his internment ceremony. All of my feelings of grief have been openly expressed and shared with others and I have a realistic image of who he was.

He was a fine man…a meek and mild man…a totally honest man…a man whose childhood Christian faith was rekindled when he married Betty. When he said grace before meals and when he prayed in church, there was no doubt in my mind that he had God's ear. His sincerity in prayer and his faith in God were undeniable. He and Betty were married twenty-six years, and with each passing year he seemed to be more and more in his prime.

Whenever my father said good-bye to me at the end of a visit during the last decade of his life, he always hugged me and whispered in my ear, "I love you."

February 6, 1997
The spring term started today. I am taking a course on marriage and family.

After class I met another student. We chatted for a while and I asked her what her religious tradition was. She said she is a "Unitarian Universalist." Since I had not heard of that, I asked her about it. She said it is a Protestant denomination which welcomes people of varying religious and spiritual beliefs. Then she took a small card out of her wallet and handed it to me saying, "We don't believe in creeds, but members of our congregations usually choose to affirm and promote seven Principles and six Sources of inspiration. They are listed on this card." I took the card and put it in my school bag. I just read it a few minutes ago. Wow, I really like what it says.

Unitarian Universalist Principles and Sources

Unitarian Universalist congregations affirm and promote seven principles:

— The inherent worth and dignity of every person;
— Justice, equity and compassion in human relations;

— Acceptance of one another and encouragement to spiritual growth in our congregations;
— A free and responsible search for truth and meaning;
— The right of conscience and the use of the democratic process within our congregations and in society at large;
— The goal of world community with peace, liberty, and justice for all;
— Respect for the interdependent web of all existence of which we are a part.

Unitarian Universalism draws from many sources:

— Direct experience of that transcending mystery and wonder, affirmed in all cultures, which moves us to a renewal of the spirit and an openness to the forces which create and uphold life;
— Words and deeds of prophetic women and men which challenge us to confront powers and structures of evil with justice, compassion, and the transforming power of love;
— Wisdom from the world's religions which inspire us in our ethical and spiritual life;
— Jewish and Christian teachings which call us to respond to God's love by loving our neighbors as ourselves;
— Humanist teachings which counsel us to heed the guidance of reason and the results of science, and warn us against idolatries of the mind and spirit;
— Spiritual teachings of earth-centered traditions which celebrate the sacred circle of life and instruct us to live in harmony with the rhythms of nature.

I am fascinated by these words and concepts. They resonate with me a lot! I will find a Unitarian Universalist church and attend a service to see how that feels to me.

April 16, 1997

A central part of the course I am taking on marriage and family involves each student getting in touch with his/her Family of Origin. One of the related assignments is for each student to have a conversation with his/her oldest living family member. In the conversation the student can use specific questions from the course materials to gather Family of Origin data. After the conversation the student can write a letter to the interviewed family member, reporting back on the content of the conversation as well as the student's analysis and response to the content. The letter is not intended to actually be sent to the family member. Instead, writing the letter is meant to be a vehicle for the student to document the data s/he received, and then write his/her reflections, analysis, and conclusions about the data.

Two days ago I spoke by phone with my eighty-three year old aunt, my mother's sister, who lives 1000 miles away. The conversation I had with her profoundly enhanced my self-understanding. I want to write the class-assigned, hypothetical letter to my aunt right now, right here, in this diary. This is a huge challenge for me. May it also be a huge blessing for me!

Dear Auntie,

I am writing to you for two reasons. First, I want to thank you for being willing to spend time with me on the phone last week in order to give me the information I need to construct a genogram for the course I am taking in seminary on marriage and the family. Second, I need to complete another assignment for the course by writing a letter to you about the content of our conversation and my thoughts about it.

In the first part of our conversation, I asked you about names and dates of our family members. Next, I asked you questions about those family members, particularly your mother and father. When I asked you to tell me about your mother - who died three weeks before I was born - you shared the following information. You said you are a lot like your mother. She was strict; she was a very good housekeeper, and she had very strong ideas about what was right, what was wrong, and what was proper. You emphasized the word "proper," explaining you and my mother were not allowed to do improper things. You mentioned you and my mother may have thought you were missing out on things as children because your mother would not let you "emulate" other children. You said you similarly taught your children not to be like other children. You also shared that niceties had to be observed in the family. An example was the white lace tablecloth which was always on the dining room table.

You said your family had more advantages than others, such as nice clothes and big cars. You said the family was very proud of having good principles and would not stoop to others' ways of living. You said your father was very smart and was respected by others for his intelligence. You mentioned your father contributed money to a local church each year, but the family never went to church. You said your mother was very proud of her Irish heritage.

You stated you believed others were not in your class - that you were above others. You said you were taught to think this way when you were a child, and you passed this way of thinking on to your children. You noted that even though you felt you were in a higher class than others, you never let others know you felt that way. You emphasized others have always respected you.

When I asked about your parents' relationship, you said your father spoiled your mother. He let her make a lot of the decisions. You said your parents did everything together. They had a 50-50 marriage, although you think your mother had the stronger personality. You mentioned your parents never disagreed in front of you and my mother. And you said your father was lost after your mother died.

When I asked how anger was handled in your family, you said it wasn't tolerated. When I asked how sadness was handled, you said your mother would "rationalize" and talk you children out of sadness. When I asked how illness was handled, you said it really wasn't much of an issue. You did mention your mother was not strong and she would take a nap every afternoon. You also acknowledged there were many anxious years when my mother became ill with cancer, and that was an appropriate response for a diagnosis of cancer at that time in history.

You spoke about the fact that you passed on to your children the belief that problems should be kept within the family and definitely not shared with others outside the family. You instructed your children to not discuss family things at school. I told you about a woman in my neighborhood when I was young who remarked to me that no one ever knew what was going on in our family.

At the end of the conversation you drew attention to the attributes of class and respect again. You reiterated that you still believe you are a class above others. And you repeated that you have been shown a lot of respect throughout your life. You said you are proud of your life.

Auntie, in the remainder of this letter, I want to reflect on how I am processing the information you gave me. This will include my reaction to our phone conversation and my analysis of the psychodynamics of our family of origin based on the data from our conversation and my life experiences. I invite you to know what is in my mind and heart by reading the rest of this letter, but I preface this invitation with the comment that my perspective on our family of origin, and my personal life values, are very different from yours. What I write may feel offensive to you although my intent is not to offend you. My intent is instead threefold: (1) to reflect on my reaction to our conversation (2) to clarify for myself what I believe the reality of our family of origin is, and (3) to share with you my ideas on our family of origin as one adult woman to another - in order that we may learn from each other and appreciate each other more.

I was shocked, upset, and sad as a result of our talk. I realize now I had expected to hear something about love, or kindness, or caring, or compassion during the conversation; but that was not the case and I was shocked by the omission. On the other hand, what you told me validated the necessity for all of the psychological and spiritual work which I have needed to do in order to move toward becoming a whole human being. Your words confirmed the insidious dysfunction in our family which wreaked incredible havoc in me for fifty years. Related to that, I literally shudder now as I understand how this dysfunction has played out not only in my life, but also in your nuclear family, and in my brother's. My awareness of this trans-generational transfer of dysfunction makes me very upset.

The sadness I have continued to feel since our conversation comes from my realization that I had an unconscious hope deep inside me which was dashed in our conversation. That hope was for the emergence of some shred of evidence my mother really was a loving, compassionate person; and therefore, she may have loved me very much. Unfortunately, I heard no such evidence; and in fact, it became obvious to me the qualities of being loving and compassionate were not prioritized in our family.

The psychodynamic attributes which you named and which seem to be highly valued by our family are class superiority, "properness," respect from others, pride, and a communication system which is closed to those outside the family. My life experiences have taught me to place value in an antithetical set of attributes including humbleness, tolerance, inclusivity, authenticity, honesty, sincerity, humility, friendship, community, caring, openness, sharing, and trust. I want to reflect on the polarity of these lists.

Class superiority is an untenable concept to me because it defies a fundamental truth of our world. All human beings are

God's children and are perfectly loved by God. When, about three years ago, I finally claimed my true identity as a beloved child of God, I became appropriately humble, more tolerant of others, and more insistent on inclusivity rather than exclusivity in all aspects of my life. These attributes are peace-giving and life-enhancing. Class superiority, on the other hand, is begotten of arrogance and excessive narcissism, both unhealthy types of self-love which over time deplete the bearers of these qualities as well as those to whom the bearers relate. I was the victim of an arrogant mother and a narcissistic husband. I know first-hand the emotional destruction which results from, and to, these types of people. Subscribing to a concept of class superiority is harmful and unnatural in my opinion.

"Properness" is an interesting concept. I believe it is a half-truth. If it is subscribed to as a sincere effort to do good things, then it has its virtue. If, on the other hand, it is done to create an impression of saintliness or superiority, then it will in time become offensive much as the Pharisees became when they created an impression of righteousness but were really hypocritical. When appearances are only for show, the richness of authenticity, honesty, and sincerity is jeopardized. The result is inevitable distancing by others based on a level of discomfort which reflects distrust. Such distancing begets fear, loneliness, and lack of personal growth.

Respect by others is not a bad attribute, but its derivation is important. I believe respect by others must be a by-product of other goals rather than a goal in and of itself. To make the respect of others a primary goal is to once again wave the flag of arrogance and narcissism. To do so prioritizes self-love above the value of a person's deeds. If someone gives and receives true friendship, respect will be present. If someone participates in the spirit of community, respect will develop. If someone cares for another out of love, or receives care from another with love, respect will flourish. Sometimes the perception of respect by others is merely the narcissistic reflection of an arrogant person's conceit. In this instance, the respect is not a reality but a codependent response to an intimidating personality. An arrogant person may perceive respect from others when in reality the response is inauthentic compliance with the intimidation "rules" of the relationship.

The attribute of pride is problematic for me. If the term is used to connote gratefully taking pleasure in one's accomplishments, then it is legitimate, I suppose. But the reality is that all we are and all we have are gifts from God. Our response to doing something well can be praise to God for giving us the ability to do that something well. Our response to having a nice physical body or a specific ethnic ancestry can be praise to God for His gifts rather than a false sense of superiority which smacks once again of arrogance and conceit. My experience has been that sincere humility and thanksgiving for my many blessings, rather than pride, revitalize me and connect me joyfully with my maker. Pride is an empty, self-limiting, and self-destroying attribute in my opinion.

A closed communication system which is put in place to lock others out is very dangerous. It, by its nature, presumes it is superior to everything without, and thereby deprives itself from receiving, exchanging, and accessing revitalizing new ways to be. A closed communication system gives silent testimony to the anxiety of the system's creator. His/her attempt to control the natural process of growth, enlightenment, and interaction with the outside reveals his/her insecurity and fear of change. Such a system is probably founded on an unconscious theology which presupposes an unloving and untrustworthy God, and a humanity which is primarily ignorant and incompetent. It has been my experience this kind of system perpetuates harmful, narrow, unenlightened, even evil ways of being because the closed ways are never challenged and thereby adapted to the real world. People who live within these systems are therefore robbed of developing their true selfhood and spirituality because they are smothered by the stagnant and confining elements within. The people within these systems ultimately become depressed and lonely as they live choked off from the light and warmth which the outside world can provide through an open system of communication and relationships.

Auntie, I have shared these thoughts with you trusting they will help you to know me a little better and to therefore appreciate what I have grown to value in my life – even if you don't agree with my thoughts. Through our conversation, I grew to appreciate how hard you have worked throughout your life to live up to your parents' high standards and to win other people's respect. Your current sense of feeling good about how you have lived your life indicates you have been successful in achieving your family's goals. I also suspect, even though we didn't talk about it, that it was very painful for you to lose my mother. She was a very strong presence and she embraced similar goals to yours. I remember the two of you were the best of friends. I can only imagine how painful your grieving process must have been after she died, and how traumatic the shift in the family dynamics must have been. I am sorry for the losses you suffered at her death.

I also want you to know your disappearing out of my life was a huge loss for me. You were my favorite aunt when I was a child and I loved you very much. Then when I was eighteen years old and needed to go to a psychiatrist, you were suddenly gone. Did you disappear because you were ashamed of me? Or was my grief over the loss of my mother too much for you to bear with me? I really would like to know why you went away. I missed you very much. Nine years after you disappeared from my life, on the afternoon and evening of my wedding day, I cried because you didn't come to the wedding even though you were invited. I felt huge hurt and abandonment at your absence.

But as you know, Betty became a wonderful stepmother for me and I was exposed to a new way of living. Together, she and Daddy created a wonderful, Christian home within which I was a primary benefactor. I received the love and compassion I needed when I was so grief-ridden and confused. And I witnessed first-hand the blossoming of my father into a differentiated, joyful, confident, and peace-filled human being within the context of a loving, Christian marriage and a value system which encouraged thanksgiving, community, fun, and service.

Then, unfortunately, an unconscious sense of familiarity with the old, arrogant, and controlling style of living, contributed to my choosing a husband who was essentially a replication of my mother. And for twenty years I existed in a closed, compassionless relationship with an arrogant, demanding man. But finally that situation was no longer acceptable to me and I left it and went to my loving friends and a nearby Christian community for nurturance. I was not disappointed. Once again, as with Dad and Betty, my needs for love, understanding and compassion were met, and the hard work of growing into my own personhood continued. And now, thanks be to God, I am very clear about my identity as a child of God, and I am living and learning and serving in the wholeness of that identity which affords me the graces of love, joy, gratitude, peace, and hope. No more is necessary.

So, Auntie, in ending this letter I want to thank you once again for being willing to share some family history with me. While I believe the "better-than-others," "appearance-oriented," and "closed" orientation to life was very toxic for me, I am choosing now to detach my disdain about this orientation from the people who taught it to me. You are my aunt. Your sister was my mother. I loved both of you very much and I gratefully hold on to the good we knew together. My days on the farm with you were wonderful times. My mother rubbing my back and singing to me at night, and sometimes holding me on her lap in the old rocking chair, were special moments of loving care which I remember and am grateful for.

Auntie, I wish you well. And I wish for you a sense of God's perfect love for you. May you experience His grace and forgiveness, His comfort and His peace.

Love,
Susan

August 14, 1997

Today was the last day of a wonderful summer course I have been taking on nonviolence.

Prior to attending the class I thought I had experienced almost no violence in my life. That is to say, physical violence had been minimal in my life – consisting of receiving a few gentle spankings from my very kind father when I was a little girl, enduring one traumatic spanking from my mother, and witnessing a school principal paddling a troublesome child when I became an elementary school teacher in the public schools.

On the first day of the course the class learned a definition for the word "violence." The definition significantly changed my perspective. "Violence is emotional, verbal, or physical behavior which dominates, diminishes, or destroys ourselves or others." Wow! That definition is much broader than just physical violence. And the class exercises helped all of us reflect on not just physical violence, but also on the significant emotional and verbal violence we have experienced - as recipients, as perpetrators, and as observers.

Overall the course was a magnificent awareness-raising experience regarding the presence of violence in our world, the presence of violence in our individual lives, and the movements and leaders who have worked and are working to bring about nonviolence in our world. This is truly important work and each of us can contribute!

December 19, 1997

I just finished a course on shame, guilt, and forgiveness. It was very worthwhile. Among many other things I learned that "guilt" is about something someone has done, and "shame" is about who someone is. I think this distinction is important because it raises consciousness about the difference between "human doing" and "human being." Human doing involves experiences in an individual's life, while human being involves an individual's identity. Andrew P. Morrison's book, *The Culture of Shame*, is a good read for understanding shame and guilt.

Robert D. Enright's "Process Model of Forgiveness," taken from the book, *Dimensions of Forgiveness*, spoke to me personally. Over the years I have struggled with the concept of forgiveness, experiencing an inability to forget - which I have linked to the concept of forgiveness. Enright's process model gave me a new step-by-step way to understand forgiveness. I want to record his process in order that I may return to it as needed.

Uncovering Phase – This phase is the most important phase. It requires the injured to look reality in the face regarding both what has happened and what reaction the injured has had. At this point the injured (1) examines his/her psychological defenses (2) confronts and releases his/her anger (3) admits his/her shame (as appropriate) (4) evaluates his/her emotional investment in the situation (5) becomes aware of how much thinking s/he is doing about the event (6) raises his/her awareness regarding comparisons of the injured to the injurer (7) realizes the permanent changes caused by the incident (8) investigates his/her feelings on a "just world" view.

Decision Phase – This phase prepares the injured to forgive and facilitates a commitment to forgive. The injured (9) considers a new and more helpful way to frame the event (10) considers forgiveness (11) makes a commitment to forgive the injurer.

Work Phase - In this phase the injured (12) considers the injurer in his/her context (13) develops a compassionate view toward the injurer (14) accepts/absorbs the pain of the event (15) forgives the injurer by giving a moral gift to him/her.

Deepening Phase – In this phase the injured becomes free of the emotional burden of the event and may extend beneficence to other similarly injured people (16).

The final assignment for the shame, guilt, and forgiveness course was to write a critical evaluation of Nathaniel Hawthorne's novel, *The Scarlet Letter*. Both Morrison's book and Enright's model helped me enormously with this assignment. I worked hard on my paper and learned a lot by writing it. Unfortunately the assignment did not include a requirement for students to write a personal reflection regarding their own history/relationship with shame, guilt, and forgiveness. In other courses, I have greatly benefitted from a requirement to write a personal reflection on the course topic(s).

March 18, 1998

Over the past year I have been attending a Unitarian Universalist (UU) church. While many elements of the Sunday morning services are similar in format to other Protestant churches (hymns, sermons, prayers, etc.), the UU services do not include the "Apostles' Creed" nor references to the Trinity (Father, Son, and Holy Ghost). God is referred to and wisdom is shared from many religious traditions as well as many spiritual and secular sources. Parishioners are invited forward each Sunday to light candles and speak of joys and concerns in their lives. Religious exploration classes for children are provided and fascinating lifelong-learning courses are offered for adults. There are numerous social functions and social justice events. Competent pastoral care offered by the minister and lay people is available and encouraged.

I have decided the UU tradition is right for me...for many reasons. The UU Principles and Sources statements resonate strongly with my values, my life experiences, and my needs. I like the "energy" of the people who attend UU churches - nonjudgmental, curious, open-minded, authentic, devoted to loving community, and committed to social justice for all.

In this spring term at seminary, I am taking an amazing course about Unitarian Universalist theologies in the United States. Not surprisingly, the many theologies we are learning about are varied in their perspectives. This phenomenon is itself very UU. And, for me, the richness of this diversity is both instructive and inspirational. Also, it is noteworthy to me that so much diversity is captured within the gracious framework of the UU Principles and Sources statements.

May 14, 1998

During this term at seminary I have been hearing about a training program to equip seminary students (and others) for hospital chaplaincy work. I find I am interested in this opportunity. Could such a training program enable me to heal from my exaggerated fears of illness and hospitals? Might hospital chaplaincy become a new vocation for me?

The training program is called Clinical Pastoral Education (CPE). It is offered by a number of hospitals around this area. Completing one CPE unit can be accomplished on a part-time basis over 8 months, or on a full-time basis over 10 weeks. To become a nationally certified Hospital Chaplain, four CPE units must be successfully completed.

Hmm…To do one part-time CPE unit, I would need to request a change from my full-time business world position to a part-time position. I have no idea if such a change is possible. If the change is possible, can I financially afford to make the change? Am I willing to take the risk of jeopardizing my corporate business world career?

There is definitely a lot to think about when considering hospital chaplaincy as a potential future vocation for myself.

September 24, 1998

Tomorrow I start my first unit of Clinical Pastoral Education (CPE). This is a nine-month, part-time, Hospital Chaplain Internship program. It includes monthly three-day training sessions, as well as weekly part-time on-the-job work as a chaplain in a hospital. There will be fifteen chaplain interns in the monthly training sessions. Each of us will be assigned to an experienced hospital chaplain who works in the surrounding area. This chaplain will supervise our weekly work in his/ her hospital setting.

I am eager to take this training…and frightened to take it. My life-long fears of illness and hospitals will definitely make this experience an enormous challenge for me.

Onward!

December 19, 1998
Whew! I have been doing part-time work in the corporate business world and part-time CPE in the religious world for twelve weeks now. I feel fortunate to be doing both.

So far in CPE I have received meaningful training each month over a three-day weekend. In the hospital setting, I have done patient visitation for at least eight hours a week. These visits are deeply meaningful to me - in spite of the anxiety I experience in the hospital setting. There are also written assignments which require a lot of reflection and thoughtful writing. So far, all of us interns have been required to write up seven patient visits, using a writing format called a "verbatim." We have also been required to read five books and write a short "reflection" on each of them. And there have been other writing assignments for reflections on our "pastoral placement" (how our hospital situation is working out), "learnings" we have experienced, and our responses to "training session topics." Each paper is read by the supervisor who writes extensive comments. These comments are enlightening and very helpful. I received (mostly) approving comments on the verbatim which follows.

CPE
VERBATIM
12/03/1998

Chaplain: Susan

Patient Date of Admission: 11/28/1998   **Service:** Oncology

Age: 68   **Gender:** M   **Status:** Married   **No. of Children:** None

Religious Preference: Catholic

Admitting Diagnosis to Hospital: Metastatic lung cancer to the brain

Factual Information: This verbatim is about the wife of the patient. I will call her "W" and the patient "H." I had met W on two previous occasions.

Patient's Initial Concern: Her husband's pain and the long period of time she and her husband had to wait until the nurse came with the pain medicine.

Pastoral Opportunity: To be present with W in her pain at watching her husband's pain, and in her anger about how long it took to get pain medicine. I hoped validating her husband's physical pain, her emotional pain, and her anger would facilitate her processing the suffering in a releasing/healing way.

ADDITIONAL INFORMATION
I first met W twenty-three days before this visit when I entered her husband's room just ahead of the arrival of his friends. I asked W if she wanted to chat with me down the hall in the lounge while her husband visited with his friends. She agreed and we had a 15 minute visit.

In that first visit, she said she doesn't usually talk with other people about her problems. "What good can it do?" she asked. She told me she is the one to whom everyone in the family turns for help. She said it makes her feel better and helps her forget her problems when she is helping others. She asked me if I thought her husband's illness could have happened in order to create quality time for them to be together. She said her husband is a typical male who doesn't share his feelings. She mentioned that her experience with bypass surgery a while back was bad but this experience is awful.

I saw W briefly ten days after our first meeting when her husband had been readmitted for a short stay and they were literally on their way out of the hospital. She said she remembered me. She seemed very agitated in the few moments I saw her, saying she couldn't wait to get out of the hospital and she never wants to come back.

PLANS

- Pray in the hospital chapel for God's presence, love, and power to enfold me, the patients, and the caregivers I would visit that day (general plan)
- Discuss W's case with my collaborative chaplain who had been seeing the couple during this admission
- Reintroduce myself to W and her husband
- Make it a point to observe the physical characteristics of the room, the patient, and W
- Make it a point to hear and address the initial concerns of the patient and W
- Provide pastoral care to the patient and W
- Take meaningful notes in reflection time after the visit
- Follow up on the visit with my supervising chaplain and any other appropriate hospital personnel

OBSERVATIONS

The room door was closed. I asked the ward secretary if I should knock and she encouraged me to do so. I knocked and W said "Come in." The patient's bed was near the door. W was seated in a chair on the other side of the bed. A mattress (where W sleeps each night) was on the floor between her chair and the outside wall of the room. An extra chair was near the foot of the bed and a vase with cut flowers was on the window ledge.

The patient (H) appeared to be asleep. He is a medium size man with a round face, dark bushy eyebrows, and medium size facial features. His almost bald head revealed a little gray hair near his temples. His denture-less mouth presented a caved in look to his face. His color was a bit ashen. His arms were under the sheet which was pulled up to his shoulders. He had an oxygen tube in his nose, and an IV stand was positioned behind W's chair.

W remained seated in her chair as I walked in. She is a short woman, probably 5', and slender. Her face is oval with balanced features and the normal lines of a woman who is 60-ish. Her predominantly gray hair has a few remaining streaks of light brown through it. It is wavy/kinky and was pulled back into a low ponytail which hung 3-4 inches down her back. She was wearing large, dark rimmed glasses and no make-up. She had dark circles under her hazel eyes which were relatively clear. She was wearing a pair of blue jeans, light yellow loafers with socks, and a colorful, flowered, long-sleeved cotton top. Her thin lips formed a straight line in an expression which seemed to show sadness. She recognized me and immediately asked me to pull up the extra chair near the foot of the bed.

THE VISIT: (C=Chaplain, W=Wife, H=Husband/Patient)

C-1   Hello, W. I am Susan, a Chaplain.

W-1   Yes, I remember you.

C-2   (I looked toward her husband who seemed to be asleep.) I came by to hear what's going on for you two today.

W-2   Pull up that chair. (She motioned toward the chair at the foot of the bed.)

C-3   (I pulled the chair away from the wall, positioning it to face her, about two feet in front of her.)

W-3   He's in pain. (She started to cry softly.) The nurse just gave him more pain medicine. It makes him sleepy. (More tears)

C-4   (I leaned forward toward her and put my hand on her knee.) This is a very difficult time for you. It's so hard to watch someone you love be in pain.

W-4   Yes. And I pressed the button over a half hour ago for the nurse, but she just came. If I were at home I would have done something right away.

C-5   You're feeling frustrated it took so long for the nurse to come, and you're angry at having to wait.

W-5   Yes...and he's not getting any better. Now it's up here. (She pointed to her temples indicating the cancer had spread to his brain.) Why did they give him chemo and all the other treatments if they weren't going to do any good?

C-6   I hear you are angry the treatments haven't helped.

W-6   Yes, I am angry. And I'm not even sure the doctor thought it would help - even though he told me we would all three fight this thing together. But the treatments haven't helped, and now he says we could try radiation up here. (She pointed to her temples again.) But radiation could make his respiration harder down the road.

C-7   So a decision needs to be made about whether or not to have radiation treatments and that is a difficult decision to make.

W-7   Yes. I just don't know what is right. H says he doesn't want to do any more treatments. It's like he's giving up. (More tears) We've fought this all along the way and now it seems like he's giving up.

C-8   You're seeing a change in H's attitude and it's very upsetting to you.

W-8   Yes. I feel like I have to make the decision because he isn't feeling well, and I think he still wants to fight even though he says he doesn't. You know how when you're feeling bad you think you don't care if you live or die, but then when you start to get better you realize you didn't know what you really wanted? I think he still wants to fight.

C-9   So even though H is saying he doesn't want to have more treatments, you're afraid he may not really know what he wants because he is feeling so badly.

W-9   Yes. You know we have always argued, and I would always put up a good argument until I was sure he really did know what he wanted. Then I would give in and let him have his way even if it wasn't what I wanted. And that was okay with me. But now, I think I have to make this decision because he doesn't know what he wants.

C-10   You feel responsible for making this decision even though H says he doesn't want more treatment.

W-10   (She starts to cry again.) I just don't want to accept it.

C-11   Accepting H really doesn't want to have more treatment is very hard for you.

W-11   Yes. (She continues to cry.)

C-12   It sounds like H has moved on to a new place which is different from where you are. It's like he has moved on to here (I swept my left hand from my right to my left in front of me) and you are still here (I moved my right hand from my right to my center).

W-12   I don't want to accept it.

C-13   (Nodding with empathy) I know you don't. You have fought so hard...

W-13   (After a pause) What stage do you think I'm at?

C-14   What stage?

W-14 In the stages of death and dying, aren't there seven stages?

C-15 Oh…Well, I do know about those stages, but I don't remember right now what they all are.

W-15 I am angry…and I don't want to accept it.

C-16 (I nodded, acknowledging her self-awareness.)

W-16 (After a brief pause) You know, sometimes I said bad things to him. Like when he'd go off to be with his friends and leave me alone. I usually didn't care that I was left alone but sometimes I would say bad things. One time I even told him I wished he was dead. (More tears)

C-17 I hear you're feeling guilty about what you said. Do you think he believed what you said?

W-17 Oh no. I even told my sister once that I said awful things to him but I knew he didn't believe them.

C-18 So you know he didn't believe what you said. You were angry at the moment and said things that you regret. Human beings do that.

W-18 You know there was a period when we went our separate ways. Do you think that this has happened because of that?

C-19 What do you think?

W-19 (Shaking her head from side to side and almost smiling) No, I don't believe that God punishes us like that.

C-20 (I nodded, acknowledging her conclusion).

W-20 You know once his business was off the ground and doing well, I decided I wanted to go to nursing school. He said that was fine, and I did. Do you think that happened in preparation for my being able to care for him in this way now?

C-21 Well, I don't have an answer to that, but I do believe from my experiences that God has a way of taking bad situations and bringing good circumstances to bear on them.

W-21 You know when I was in nurse's training there was a man in the hospital whose wife was in a terrible condition, and he insisted that she be kept alive. He was a rich man who needed to keep her alive until some legal things were set up in his favor. It was terrible. All of us nurses met with the supervisor about it because it upset us so much. It was just awful to keep her alive in that condition. I never thought I would feel that way, but I did. And it wasn't even my own family.

C-22 Seeing that situation made you feel differently than you thought you would.

W-22 Yes...You know, I've signed a DNR.

C-23 (I nodded in acknowledgment.)

W-23 And now I feel I have to make the decision about the radiation. (Pause) The doctor says I am giving him mixed messages.

C-24 Hmm...(I nodded again.)

W-24 (After a pause then starting to cry again) This morning my husband and I both cried together.

C-25 You both felt very sad...I'm glad the two of you can be together and share your feelings. That's very special. (After a pause) Would you like me to say a prayer with you now?

W-25 Yes.

C-26 (I moved my chair a little closer to her and took both of her hands. I took a deep breath in, let it out slowly, and prayed.) Oh good and gracious, God, we invite your presence with us now, and we ask you to surround W with your love. Grant her your guidance as she faces difficult decisions and help her to know you are always with her, to comfort her and sustain her. Bless the special time W and H are sharing now and give to both of them your peace which passeth all understanding. In Jesus' name we pray. Amen. (We both stood up and I hugged W.)

W-26 Thank you very much.

C-27 You're welcome. I'll stop by to see you tomorrow.

W-27 Thank you.

C-28 Bye.

January 14, 1999

Today I handed in a Critical Incident Report to the priest who is my CPE supervisor. The report follows. It speaks for itself.

CLINICAL PASTORAL EDUCATION
Critical Incident Report

Date: 1/14/1999
Chaplain: Susan
Overview of the Report: The Re-Visitation of an Adolescent Trauma

I have found great meaning in the visitations I have had with patients during the first half of this CPE unit. I believe I have been able to connect with the patients in a deeply spiritual way, and in a very pastoral way. I have been present with them in their pain, their fear, their anger, and their hope; and I have felt privileged to be present with them in all of these situations. Yet, the experience in the hospital has been filled with anxiety for me. Each time I have climbed the stairs to my assignment on the Medical/Surgical floor, I have needed to summon every bit of courage I had to endure the fear which filled me. How could this dichotomy exist? How could I value the interaction with the patients so much, and simultaneously be in a state of acute anxiety? I found out part of the answer nine days ago.

At the "Check-In" time with a community-of-interest business and spirituality group I participate in, I said things were going fine for me. Then another member of the group asked me, "How is the chaplain internship going?" Knowing it was safe – even encouraged - in this group to be honest, I admitted I was very disappointed in myself that I continued to be so anxious in the hospital environment. Another group member then said, "What is it like for you to be there?" Surprised by his directness and gentle probing, I began to tell how it felt to me. I described how I climb the stairs to the Medical/Surgical floor and then upon seeing the shiny linoleum floor of the Medical/Surgical hallway, I instantly become very anxious. And as I spoke, I could see the shiny floor of the hallway in my mind's eye; and my palms began to perspire.

Then someone asked, "What are you afraid of?" I replied that I didn't know. At that point, the woman beside me (Darlene), who is a professional therapist, invited me to close my eyes, breathe deeply, and stay with the feeling of fear. I closed my eyes and the fear swept over me like a wave. I began to cry and tremble. Darlene then gently asked, "What is going on for you now?" The image in my mind went from the hospital hallway where my chaplain assignment is to the hospital hall – and then room – where I stood as a fourteen year old girl, seeing my mother for the last time as she was dying of cancer. Through my tears and trembling I described how she looked with her mouth hanging open and her eyes half-closed, propped up in bed, and surrounded by an oxygen tent. My whole body shook in fear and horror.

Then Darlene gently guided me to stay with my fear, to keep breathing, and to keep describing what was going on for me. She asked me again what I was feeling. From the depths of my being I blurted out, "I didn't want her to die."

I started sobbing and members of the group got up from their chairs in the circle to come close to me and comfort me. I stood up and four or five of them surrounded me, holding me in their embrace. One woman (Jane) who was directly in front held me in such a loving embrace, I could feel her energy field of love flowing into me like a wonderful, full river. I felt almost afloat in the love that surrounded me. Yet simultaneously in my imagination, I was still in the hospital room with my mother. There I stood, reliving the horrible scene and feeling deep emotional pain and fear, but at the same time feeling engulfed in love and support. Darlene asked me who else was there in the hospital room with me. I said I didn't know. I sensed that someone else was there, but I couldn't see his/her face in my mind.

After what seemed like several more minutes, my fear suddenly began to subside and the trembling began to diminish. And then it stopped. I was still standing in the hospital room with my mother, in my mind, but I had become calm. That was a powerful moment for me...And along with the sense of calm, I continued to be aware of the gentle, rich love that surrounded me, emanating from the group members. I gladly lingered in their loving, healing embrace.

Then gradually I opened my eyes. The group members made sure I was all right before I sat down, and then they returned to their seats. I slowly looked up and around the circle at them. I have never seen such sincere compassion and love as I saw in each person's eyes. They were literally holding me in their collective, loving gaze. I was awestruck and filled with gratitude.

The next day was my chaplain visitation day. I went to the hospital wondering if the experience I had had with the group would have an impact on my way of being in the hospital. Before I went out on the Medical/Surgical floor, I went to the hospital chapel. I asked God to be present with me in my ministry that day, and to help me integrate the healing experience I had had with the group, into my presence at the hospital as a chaplain. I called back the sense of guidance I had felt from Darlene, the sense of unrestrained love I had felt from Jane and the others who held me, the sense of transformation from terror to calmness I had felt as I relived the traumatic scene with my mother, and the sense of awe and gratitude I had felt when I opened my eyes and saw the sincerity and compassion with which the group members were all attending to me. I held all of those beautiful feelings in my being and asked God to bless them and integrate them inside me. Then I asked God to bless each of the members of the group as I saw each one of them in my mind's eye.

From the chapel I went to the Medical/Surgical floor. I entered the hall very slowly, intentionally noticing all of the aspects of the environment. I noticed the shiny floor, and I mentally acknowledged its previous role as a trigger for my anxiety. I noticed the smells of antiseptics and other hospital odors which are such a poignant part of the environment. I felt the too warm climate and the accompanying stagnant, and seemingly smothering air which hangs motionlessly in the hall. I passed the IV poles, and the sterile gloves, and the heart monitors – all of the intimidating medical equipment...But my hands did not perspire; and my muscles did not tighten; and I did not become more and more anxious. Instead, I was calmly present in the environment while being acutely aware of its many here-to-fore threatening elements – elements which were part of the reality, but which no longer seemed threatening to me.

I reached the nurses' station and I was still okay. I was still calm. I was not anxious. I was ready to begin my work – and this time I was ready to begin it without fear.

I worked all day, and the fear did not return. I was overjoyed and full of gratitude for my friends and for God's grace.

February 5, 1999

Today at the beginning of our monthly CPE 3-day training meeting, I handed in a second Critical Incident Report. This report tells about the totally unexpected death of a very close friend of mine. Davida and I met several years ago at the company where we both have worked. I am in shock, and I am grieving. The Critical Incident Report follows.

CLINICAL PASTORAL EDUCATION
Critical Incident Report

Date: 2/5/1999
Chaplain: Susan
Overview of the Report: The Death of a Close Friend

On Sunday evening, January 24, 1999, my phone rang. The husband of my close friend, Davida, said, "Susan, this is Danny Nilstrom." "Hi Danny. How are you?" I asked. "I'm not very good" he said. Hearing the pain in his voice I then asked, "What's wrong, Danny?" I expected to hear that something had happened to their three year old son. Instead, Danny softly said, "Davida is dead."

Those three words seemed to chisel themselves into my consciousness. "Oh Danny...I am so sorry," I responded. Danny then told me Davida died in her sleep the night before - although she had not been sick, and the cause of her death was still not known. I don't remember the details of what else we said to each other, but we both cried and I tried to say something "chaplain-ish." Yet, I needed a chaplain too. When I hung up the phone, I sat in shock. I saw Davida clearly in my mind and prayed for her. I couldn't call my friends from work for quite a while. When I did, one became hysterical. The others were in shock just as I was. I thought of Danny, and his little son, and Davida's Mother, Esther, who lives in a mother-in-law apartment in Danny and Davida's home. It was like a bad dream, a very bad dream. I didn't sleep much that night.

The next day I got on the commuter train, planning to study the client materials I needed to be familiar with for a consulting meeting that morning. But my mind went to Davida. And a poem about her began to form in mind. So I put my client materials away and started to write what was in my heart. I didn't finish the poem by the time I got to the end of the train ride, but I felt some better. Putting my thoughts in verse was a way for me to begin processing my grief.

The wake for Davida was several miles from my home, a messy drive in the snow. Two friends from work rode with me. I was glad for their company. In my mind I was dreading seeing Davida's body. I knew that would be very hard for me.

A steady stream of mourners poured into the funeral home. Danny embraced me in tears and then said, "I guess God really wanted her." I thought to myself, "If that thought helps you now, that is good." I asked Danny how he was doing. He said a calm had come over him and right then he was okay. I nodded, acknowledging his comment and then moving on as the line behind me was enormous.

The casket was closed. Two beautiful pictures of Davida were displayed near the casket. She was so lovely, alive and in photos. I knelt at the small kneeling rail in front of the casket. Prayers came to me. I don't remember them now.

As we drove home, I realized I was very disappointed the casket was closed. As much as I dreaded to see Davida dead, I also needed to see Davida dead. I needed to see that it was true. I wanted to have that image in my mind too. It needed to be part of my acceptance.

My work colleagues rode with me again the next day to the funeral. We joined others from the company in the church. Stories about Davida were told in hushed tones. The colleague behind me told a funny story about skiing with Davida. Another woman spoke of Davida's support when she miscarried twin babies six months before. I held the hand of the woman next to me, the friend who had become hysterical when I called her.

The casket was carried in. Danny and his family, and Davida's brother and her family, followed in pure solemnity. Davida's mother was not there. She was not at the wake either. I kept thinking about her. I knew I couldn't begin to imagine the horror she must be experiencing.

The service was a huge disappointment to me. I grew angrier and angrier as it continued. A Rabbi, who was a neighbor of Danny and Davida, read a short passage from the Old Testament. Then Davida's nephew – who was probably ten years old – read a three-sentence letter to his Aunt Davida. But the only reference the priest made to Davida, or at least the only one I can remember, was asking Jesus to forgive her sins. I was furious. As the Mass was given I looked at the casket off to the side. It wasn't even center stage! Where were the words of acknowledgment and celebration of the wonderful, beautiful person Davida was? Why was the service all about Jesus Christ when it was Davida's funeral? I was beside myself with the inadequacy of this service. Didn't the priest know how special she was, not only to me but to the rows and rows of people who drove miles on this snowy day to mourn her passing AND celebrate her life? Perhaps the familiarity of the Catholic Mass is comforting to Catholics, but where is the part of the service which names the shock and the dismay of this occasion? And where was the healing part of the service which reinforced the wonderful, beautiful memories of Davida's very special life? If not then at that service, when will the shock and the pain of Davida's death begin to be integrated with the appreciation and love for her and her wonderful life? Shouldn't this service and this representative of God who is leading the service be the initial and prime facilitator of this important integration?

We drove to the cemetery and walked up a small hill to the gravesite which had a tent over it. It was very cold and the wind made it feel bitter. The tent was barely big enough to cover the mourners. Someone, I guess the priest, said a few words. At least these were compassionate words, words which acknowledged the people there and the loss we were suffering. And there were words to express the family's gratitude for the support of those present. And then in a few brief moments, we were all walking back down the hill in the cold and snow. I had no sense of having participated in an adequate ending for my friend.

The woman who had been hysterical when I called her, wanted to have lunch. We dropped our other colleague off and found a place for the two of us to eat. She felt unsatisfied with the service too. She said that in her Greek faith tradition, everyone at the gravesite is given a long-stemmed flower and then each mourner files by the casket, lays the flower on the casket, and has an opportunity to say goodbye to the deceased. She missed that ritual. It sounded like a good ritual to me. I could see how it would provide an appropriate ending, and a chance for mourners to say an individual goodbye while in a community setting.

The next day I spent several hours finishing my poem. I don't have a clue how to write poetry, but I needed to write this poem. When I finished it, I called a friend to share it with her. She encouraged me to send it to Danny. I did.

Davida

My beautiful friend Davida has left this earthy place
How could she go so suddenly?
How could she go so soon?
Images of her being are so clear within my mind
Her bright brown eyes
Her wonderful smile
Her love of fun and beauty
She touched so many with her light

With love
With wisdom
And joy
The loss is great for those who remain
It's so hard to say goodbye
But wasn't her life a life of true beauty?
Wasn't her life a life of real love?
Won't the love seeds she planted continue to grow
Even as she looks down from above?
My beautiful friend Davida has left this earthly place
Her experience of human life has just come to an end
I know her soul lives on in its eternal grand existence
And I know her leaving here is just a passing, brief Amen

A week later on Sunday night the phone rang. It was Davida's mother. She said she was calling to thank me for the poem, that it was just wonderful. She said she wanted to have it framed and she wanted to make copies for her family and friends. She said she had only been able to call one other person, but she had to call me because the poem meant so much to her. We talked for quite a while and she cried a lot. I was glad I had had chaplain training. Even though I didn't cry during the conversation, it was helpful for me to be in touch with her and to share, and I mean share, her grief. A few days later she called again and asked me to go to the company's office and put a copy of the poem on the bulletin board for others to see. And she asked if I would write a note to thank everyone at the company for the unbelievable outpouring of love that she and her family were receiving. She cried a lot during that conversation too but she also began to share memories about Davida. Some of them were funny memories. It was good for me to be part of that sharing, and it was good for me to be able to help Esther by putting the poem and a thank you note on the company bulletin board.

I called Esther the third time we spoke in order to share what I had written as a thank you note for her. This time we actually laughed together as she told more stories about Davida. Esther is an amazing woman, so in touch with her feelings and so full of love. I knew this was true from what Davida had told me about her mother. What a privilege it is for me to be getting to know her firsthand now. It is obvious to me where Davida got her good start. Before we hung up, Esther said she wanted to send me two things: a picture of Davida in her wedding dress, and a small sterling silver bookmark Davida gave her a while ago. She said she wanted me to have them to remember Davida. They arrived this week.

The Wednesday after Davida died, I went to the hospital to do my chaplain visitations. Arlene, another CPE student, arrived just as I arrived. She encouraged me to talk about my loss. I told her I had been wondering on the way over in the car if life is really just a lousy joke. I told her I was tired of illness and death. I told her I didn't want to do illness and death anymore, that I just wanted to enjoy what is good about life now. We talked, and I cried, for quite a while. Then with Arlene's guidance, I began to realize a key reason why Davida's death feels so terrible to me. Not only is her death tragic, not only are her family members devastated, not only will I miss seeing and being with the beautiful bright light that Davida was in my life. In addition to all of that, I have lost an anchor in my life. Davida was an anchor of wisdom for me in the area of character discernment regarding the men in my life. She intuitively had wisdom about men and relationships which I don't have. I trusted her wisdom in this area. Now this source of grounding for me is gone. Hopefully, what I learned from Davida will remain with me in the future.

I haven't felt like visiting in the hospital since Davida died. I've stayed away. I fear I will find I have regressed back to the anxious state I was in before the wonderful healing experience I had in the beginning of January. I am afraid the healing experience was so fresh and so fragile it has probably lost its effect since the shock of Davida's death. The woman who helps supervise the CPE program seemed to comprehend the situation well when she suggested Davida's death may have re-traumatized me. That sounds "right on" to me. I just don't want to go there again – to the anxious state. It's just too overwhelming. I fear it will be more than I can bear, and I am tempted to avoid finding out.

February 20, 1999

I need to force myself into looking at the history of my illness phobia. Sigh…

I was three years old when my mother was diagnosed with breast cancer. The doctors gave her six months to live. She then embarked on a full-scale assault to beat the cancer. She traveled to New York City to meet with a specialist. She had a radical mastectomy and a hundred x-ray treatments. She had my father build her an "Accumulator" which was a box she could sit in. It had steel wool and other materials in the walls which were somehow supposed to create a healing field of energy which her body would absorb by sitting in it. She took me with her several times to a doctor's office where she would sit and inhale a brownish substance out of a hand-held inhaler.

But the support system she really put her faith in was a religious sect she read about in a flyer which came in the mail. After reading the flyer she sent for the sect's materials. The sect was located far away from our home. It had a church building in a big city and a convention center in an isolated area 100 miles away from the church. The founder of the sect was a European man who had been a newspaper writer. When he was on an assignment in Tibet he became ill with malaria. Some Tibetans took him to their Buddhist temple and the guru in the temple taught the European man how to heal himself. Some years later he arrived in the United States to found a new religion. He called the religion a science. Practicing the science included saying affirmations, doing breathing exercises and meditations, chanting, and following a vegetarian diet.

My mother became enamored with the materials she received in the mail. She also became enamored with the founder of the religious sect who had written the materials. She read and practiced the materials faithfully and she began to frequently correspond with the founder. Five years later our family-of-four traveled to the sect's convention center for a two-week convention. Two years after that our family traveled once again to attend our second two-week convention. And in another two years my mother sent my brother and me to our third two-week convention.

The conventions had three practice sessions a day. The attendees sat in stocking feet on chairs arranged in a large circle. The sect's founder sat cross-legged in the center of the group facing a large gong and dressed in a flowing gold robe. He taught and led the affirmations, breathing exercises, meditations, and chanting sessions.

My mother believed she healed herself from her breast cancer by practicing the sect's techniques. Then ten years after her initial diagnosis she was diagnosed with lung cancer. She died six months later. Two days before she went back to the hospital to die, she called me over to her and told me she could have healed herself again but she was just too tired to do it.

So, what does all of this have to do with my exaggerated fear of illness? Well, I suspect quite a lot. I remember my mother's sister (my aunt) telling me two things after my mother died. She said there was a lot of anxiety in our family during the years after my mother was diagnosed with breast cancer. She also told me about a phone call she received after my mother's obituary appeared in the paper. The phone call was from Mrs. Biggs who was my babysitter when I was three years old. (I loved Mrs. Biggs who was 68 years old, wore her white hair up in a bun, and probably filled the role of a grandmother for me since my mother's mother died three weeks before I was born.) After extending her sympathy to my aunt on the phone, Mrs. Biggs told my aunt a little story. She said she was staying with me when I was three years old and my mother went off to the hospital to have the mastectomy. I asked her if she would take care of me if my "Mommy" didn't come back from the hospital. Mrs. Biggs then told my aunt she pushed me away because she was afraid I would become too dependent on her.

Sigh…It becomes more and more clear to me how I could have learned to be dreadfully fearful of illness and abandonment at a very young age.

March 2, 1999

Dear God,

Over the past week I have written many times, trying to be in touch with my feelings regarding (1) the re-visitation of my mother dying, (2) Davida's death, and (3) my phobia about illness. Oh! It has been too much. I opened myself up for way, way too much emotional processing without adequate support.

I guess I got tempted to do everything I felt I could do to get on the other side of all three things in an effort to finish the CPE unit. But God, it didn't work. I have over-taxed my emotional system and I am truly reeling.

My ego wants me to conquer my CPE fears. My soul wants me to lighten up and chill out for a while. What a struggle I have taken on. It may be an important struggle for me to get over my extreme fear of illness, but it seems to me right now that finishing this CPE unit is not what I should do. CPE is too much self-imposed torture for me right now.

So how does quitting feel? Strangely, I guess it feels like leaving Dean – not what I intended, but what developing circumstances indicate is best for me.

Oh God, forgive me for not being strong enough to continue in CPE. I obviously want to finish it but my whole being is saying "NO." "GIVE ME REST FROM THIS; GIVE ME JOY; GIVE ME BEAUTY; GIVE ME HAPPINESS, AND LOVE."

Is it enough for me to respond to these needs of my body and soul? <u>I feel I cannot do otherwise and survive.</u> I choose survival, God. Help me, I pray, to accomplish survival and to still be in right relationship with You. I do not want to let You down. I hope my making this choice is <u>not</u> letting You down, God. Please stay with me. I need You.

Susan

March 10, 1999

Today I met with my CPE supervisors. I told them I need to leave the program and work with a phobia specialist who will help me get over my exaggerated fear of illness. They both wanted me to stay in the program. They said they think I am a natural for chaplaincy and they reminded me I am very close to finishing the unit - having already finished 2/3 of it. I was pleased with their affirmations of me; yet I told them I just can't do it right now. They were kind and, ultimately, accepting of my decision.

I am relieved, and I <u>will</u> find a phobia specialist.

June 24, 1999

This month I started working with a phobia specialist. She seems a little too "New Age" for me. For example, she uses channeling with her clients. The last time I saw her she decided to summon my mother through channeling. She did this after verifying through muscle testing of me that the "body" of the problem between my mother and me was in me – that I am carrying the preponderance of a burden. So my mother "came" to the session and I was intent on forgiving her in order to move past the block my anger and hatred toward her have caused me over recent years. But the phobia specialist received a message from my mother that <u>she</u> wanted to forgive <u>me</u> for criticizing her. The specialist said that by its own volition the forgiveness became two-sided. As I became aware of this surprise, I realized I had been carrying a lot of guilt for criticizing my mother even while I have needed to criticize her. And during the session with the phobia specialist my need to criticize my mother seemed to vanish and I was able to forgive her.

However, I do not place a lot of credence in the channeling process. Nor do I experience this phobia specialist as trustworthy. I will continue to see her for a while longer in order to find out what else she thinks or suggests.

November 30, 1999

Dear Diary,

It has been a very long time since I have written. I have done a lot of corporate business world work and now I want to finish the CPE unit I started and couldn't finish.

A week ago I called the man who was my supervisor in the CPE program. I asked him if I could join his current group, beginning in January, in order to finish the CPE unit I started with him. He was very glad to hear from me and very kind and thoughtful. However, he said his current CPE unit is full and he can't add me to that group. Then he quickly told me he knows of a new CPE unit starting up in January at a city nearby. He gave me the name and phone number for the supervisor of that program.

I spoke with the supervisor and liked him. He said he had space for me. I told him about the first CPE unit I tried and why I needed to leave it. Then I asked him if I could still join his group, given my history of extreme fear in the first CPE unit. To my relief he said, "Yes, of course. It's just more grist for the mill." Whew, his words make me feel relieved and hopeful. Maybe I can do this after all. I certainly hope so!

February 15, 2000
Last week I started a CPE unit in a neighboring city. I like the supervisor a lot. The group is smaller than the last group I was in and I like the group members. Today I turned in an assignment called the Personal Learning Contract. It follows:

PERSONAL LEARNING CONTRACT

Overall Learning Goal: To become a Chaplain

Personal Objective: To become more comfortable in the hospital setting.

Accomplished by: (1) Paying attention to my feelings of fear, articulating them, and reflecting on them (in writing and interactively with my Supervisor and intern colleagues) in order to release previous traumas and limiting beliefs. (2) Believing the scarred places which hold/held my traumas and limiting beliefs will be flooded with God's healing, loving, and light-filled presence.

Professional Objective: To become a competent pastoral caregiver in the hospital setting.
Accomplished by: Visiting patients, interacting with hospital staff, writing Verbatims, learning in supervisory sessions, and participating in group interpersonal sessions.

Theological Objective: To be a spiritual light and bring people to God.
Accomplished by: Practicing loving intention and attunement to my inner wisdom of divine guidance.

February 22, 2000
Today I turned in the first verbatim for my new supervisor. The document follows.

VERBATIM
2/22/2000

Chaplain: Susan
Patient Date of Admission: 1/28/2000   **Unit:** Transitional Care
Age: 80   **Sex:** F   **Marital Status:** Divorced   **No. of Children:** 2
Religious Preference: Greek Orthodox
Admitting Diagnosis: Severe complicated knee fracture
Patient's Primary Concern: "I'm too old to start over."
Length of Visit: 25 minutes

PLANS

(1) Re-introduce myself to the secretary on the floor and inform her I will be visiting patients for a couple of hours.
(2) Ask the secretary if there are any patients whom she thinks might benefit from a chaplain visit.

III

(3) Walk up and down the corridors of the unit once to get a feel for the environment and to scan the rooms for patients who appear to be available for a chaplain visit.

(4) Based on my interaction with the secretary and my scan of the unit, select a first patient to visit who is in need of support.

OBSERVATIONS

I entered a semi-private room. The bed near the door was empty although it was obvious there was a patient assigned to that bed who was temporarily out of the room. Other than two small plants on the windowsill the room had a utilitarian appearance.

The patient assigned to the second bed was sitting up in a chair by her bed near the center of the room. She was a woman in her late seventies to early eighties with gray hair which was cut in a bob about chin length. She was short in stature, probably 5 feet tall, and of moderate weight for her height. Her eyes were hazel and seemed troubled; her skin was wrinkled but had a healthy color; her mouth appeared to be denture-less; she did not wear make-up. She was dressed in cotton slacks and a short sleeve cotton blouse. A brace extended from her ankle to her knee over the slacks of her right leg.

The patient was listening to a man's voice on a transistor radio, which was lying on the bedside table by the side of her chair. She looked up at me questioningly as I approached.

THE VISIT (C=Chaplain, P=Patient, S=Patient's Roommate, OT=Occupational Therapist)

C-1   Hello. Are you S?

P-1   No.

C-2   Oh…(After looking again at the census) Are you P?

P-2   Yes.

C-3   Hello P, my name is Susan. I am a chaplain in the hospital.

P-3   (P looked at me but did not speak.)

C-4   I came by to see how you are doing today.

P-4   Not very well.

C-5   Not very well.

P-5   (P continued to look at me but did not speak.)

C-6   (Pause) So you are having a bad day?

P-6   (P turned off the transistor radio and looked right at me but didn't speak.)

C-7   (I noticed what looked like a small tear in the corner of P's eye in response to my question about her having a bad day.) You look troubled.

P-7   (P began to cry.) I am too old to begin all over again.

C-8   Begin all over again? What does that mean?

P-8   (P pointed to the brace on her leg and then held her leg as if it were painful.) I will have to learn to walk all over again and I am too old to do that. (More tears)

C-9   You sound discouraged.

P-9   Yes. Today I had a different occupational therapist and she worked me too hard and then told me I needed to work harder so they could get me out of here.

C-10   So you had a new person for occupational therapy and she worked you too hard?

P-10   Yes. I want K back. I want to talk to K.

C-11   K is your former occupational therapist and you want to talk to her?

P-11   Yes, and I need to get out of these clothes and get back into bed. They made me get dressed and sit up here today and my leg is hurting. (At this point an aide walks into the room and asks P how she is doing. P tells the aide she wants to get back in bed, and the aide says she will get someone to help put P back in bed.)

P-12   I want to talk to K. (The aid says she will get K.)

S-1   (At that point P's roommate was wheeled back into the room. I introduced myself as a chaplain and the roommate responded cordially. She looked over and saw P crying quietly.) P is having a bad day.

C-12 Yes. She is discouraged.

S-2 Well, this isn't a good day for her, but she has made a lot of progress this week. I have seen it with my own eyes. (Speaking to P) Last week you couldn't walk at all and look what you did today. (P listens but doesn't respond.)

C-13 (Speaking to S) So you feel P has been making progress?

S-3 Oh my yes. She is just having a bad day today. We all have those.

C-14 (Turning to P) S thinks you have made progress. (P seems to take that witness in. Then aides arrive to put her back in bed. P looks at me.)

C-15 I will stay right here until they are through.

P-13 Thank you.

C-16 (While I waited, I chatted with S who was in good spirits and very talkative. She told me she was a United Methodist and then told me about her parish. After 5 minutes the aides pushed the curtain back and P was lying in her bed dressed in a hospital johnny.) Does that feel better now?

P-14 Not a lot.

C-17 Hmm…

P-15 I keep praying to Mary but she doesn't hear my prayers. (She looks into my eyes and starts to cry.)

C-18 (Taking her hand) I can see it feels that way to you.

OT-1 (K entered and greeted P. K and I introduced ourselves to each other. I mentioned P wanted to talk to her because she felt she had been pushed too hard by another OT that day. Then K began a discussion with P, acknowledging P's concerns and presenting her with options for where she could go when she would leave the hospital. K was compassionate, professional, and very competent. She met P where she was emotionally, and she realistically discussed what was happening and what could happen in the future. During the discussion, I pulled a chair up beside the bed, being physically present in the discussion but letting K and P do all of the talking. At the end of the discussion, P was still distraught, but she was obviously thinking about the content of the discussion. She was beginning to look exhausted from her emotional upheaval as well.)

C-19   (I took P's hand again and she put her other hand over my hand.) You look like you are tired and could lie back and rest now. (P lay back in the bed a little more.) I need to move along, but I wonder if you would like me to say a prayer with you before I go?

P-16   Yes.

C-20   Then let us be in an attitude of prayer together. (Still holding her hand) Oh Good and Gracious God...(to my surprise P began to repeat after me each phrase I said).

P-17   Oh Good and Gracious God...

C-21   We invite your presence now with P...(she repeated)

C-22   Surround her, we pray, with your healing love...(she repeated)

C-23   And grant her the courage and strength she needs...(she repeated)

C-24   At this difficult time...(she repeated)

C-25   Bless her, as well, with your healing peace...(she repeated)

C-26   In Jesus' name we pray...(she repeated)

C-27   Amen (she repeated)

P-25   (Opening her eyes and looking at me) Thank you.

C-28   You're welcome. I am glad I got to be with you today.

P-26   What is your name?

C-29   Susan

P-27   Susan. Thank you.

C-30   You're welcome. God Bless.

March 7, 2000
Today at CPE in the intern sharing session, I shared a Critical Incident Report which I had written (rather than a verbatim). The report speaks for itself.

CPE
CRITICAL INCIDENT REPORT
MARCH 7, 2000

CHAPLAIN: Susan

OVERVIEW OF THE REPORT

This report is about a significant personal healing experience which occurred for me in connection with my current CPE experience. While the incident occurred at my home at the end of a CPE day, its triggers were:

- The CPE supervisory session held the week before
- Listening to another intern's Verbatim report earlier that day
- Being in the clinical setting that day

The incident relates to a CPE Critical Incident Report which I wrote on February 25, 1999. Both this report and the prior Critical Incident Report attest to progressive healing experiences which I have undergone as I try to get free of a deep adolescent trauma and related limiting beliefs about illness.

TRIGGERS FOR THE INCIDENT

I think there were three primary triggering events which contributed to the onset of the critical incident presented in this report.

1) At my first supervisory session in this CPE unit, I spoke openly about my fear of hospitals and my desire to work through that

fear. My supervisor listened intently and then reflected back to me that when I visit patients in the hospital I am at some level, once again visiting my mother (which was a traumatic experience for me when I was fourteen and she was dying of cancer). I had not thought of my fear experiences in quite that way before and my supervisor's comment resonated with me and helped me see more clearly a significant element of the fear reaction I have in the hospital setting. My supervisor also understood that I was having less of a sense of anxiety about being in this particular hospital setting than the hospital I was in a year ago because this hospital setting is not as similar to the hospital my mother was in. And my supervisor asked me if I knew about "Cognitive Therapy" which he suggested might be of help to me as a tool for working through my exaggerated fear.

2) On the day of the incident, at the small group verbatim session, an intern colleague described an intense situation with an HIV patient. I asked him if he felt afraid in the situation (which is the feeling I knew I would have had). He said "no," that he instead felt very sad for the patient and he was at a loss for words to use with him. When I heard this response to my question, I realized once again that my consistent reaction of fear in such situations is abnormal. Additionally, at that moment I remembered the week before when the small group was talking among ourselves and I asked the others how they dealt with their own intense feelings when someone is terminally ill or dying right before their eyes. None of the other three people responded by talking about how they dealt with their fear in such a situation. I realized that fear was not a primary emotion for them in these circumstances.

3) Also on the day of the incident because I had a cold and thought I should not visit patients, I chose to read some charts and get

better acquainted with how to do tasks at this hospital. While reading the charts, I read one for a patient who had advanced HIV/AIDS. As I read the chart I paused to imagine what it would be like to go into that patient's room. A familiar phobic feeling of fear began to sweep over me. Aware the fear was happening, I decided to observe whether or not I had any sense I was also re-experiencing going into my mother's hospital room so many years before. I was. I was indeed experiencing what my supervisor had suggested. I was startled by the awareness. I sat there for a few moments aware of both the current sense of anticipatory fear and the sense of relived fear. After a few more moments I decided I couldn't read any more charts at that time. Instead, I needed to leave the hospital. I also knew I needed to deal with my raised consciousness sooner rather than later.

THE INCIDENT

An hour or so after dinner that night I realized it was time for me to address all that was welling up in me. That is, I knew I needed to let those feeling which were right under the surface come out. So I decided to sit down at the computer and "write them" out of me. I wrote: "…the process of visiting each patient is for me the process of going into the room to see my mother when she was dying. That horrible scene of her lying propped up in bed, in an oxygen tent, with her mouth hanging open, and her eyes half closed is still extraordinarily vivid to me after 41 years. And also extraordinarily vivid to me are the feelings of sheer terror I had at the moment I saw her like that…"

Then tears began to fill my eyes. I got up from the computer and decided to use the body "tapping" techniques which I have been learning from a phobia specialist to release trapped trauma imprints from my body. For an hour and a half I proceeded to intentionally relive that horrible experience over and over again, until I could remain calm when I replayed it in my mind. I sobbed in terror for quite a while (constantly using the tapping techniques) and then I began to articulate aloud what the feelings and thoughts were behind the terror.

I spoke aloud that seeing my mother dying was the worst thing that could ever have happened to me. I verbalized that I had feared she would die since I was three years old when she first got cancer. I spoke of my having a very unhealthy, symbiotic relationship with her. (I was totally dependent on her emotionally.) And then I began to feel and articulate that I had experienced her death as somehow my death too…that my sole identity in life had been as her daughter. And when she died I lost my identity and my purpose for living. The only purpose for my life had been to make my mother OK by my being a high performance, low maintenance, and perfect daughter – a living testimony to her perfect child-rearing techniques. I spoke of how that day as I stood in her hospital room, it was for me as if I were a leaf on a tree which was being chopped down. I had done all I could to make her OK and she was still dying. And the teachings of the religious cult which she believed in and taught me (that human beings are God in human form and can totally control their health and their life successes by faithfully practicing the breathing exercises and meditations of the cult) were being invalidated right before my eyes. I couldn't bear the reality of her death and I couldn't bear the obvious invalidity of her beloved religious cult.

Next, I spoke of the three-and-a half years after my mother died during which I continued to live to glorify her memory, practicing the cult's teachings faithfully and crying myself to sleep night after night after night…alone. I spoke of how I went off to college and became overwhelmed with depression and then my family doctor recommended a psychiatrist. I recounted how at 18 years of age I began a long, long process to detach from my mother and create my own identity and life purpose. I essentially talked my way through a psychological life review of my relationship with my mother.

Toward the end of the hour and a half, with calm setting in, I lifted up my prior feelings of terror to God in prayer. I asked that the places in my body and in my being which had held the terror be healed. I asked that the pattern of my experiencing each patient I visit as my mother be broken. I asked that any possible pattern of feeling unhealthily and symbiotically linked to the patients be broken. And I prayed that the terrorizing feelings I had released be replaced with a sense of calm, love, compassion and service which will serve me well and the patients I visit. I prayed I may know and remember when I am in the role of chaplain that I am a mature, fifty-five year old woman who has been trained well (in life and in school) to do chaplain work.

Two days later I returned to the hospital and visited five patients. The exaggerated fear was gone.

Thanks be to God. May the healing continue. Amen

April 3, 2000
Tomorrow at CPE I will turn in the following Theological Reflection which I just finished preparing.

CPE
THEOLOGICAL REFLECTION
"TOWARD A THEOLOGY OF ILLNESS"
APRIL 4, 2000

CHAPLAIN: Susan

THE MINISTERIAL PROCESS

Because I am working as a hospital chaplain, I believe it is important for me to reflect on my personal theology of illness. I need to reflect on the meaning which I attach to illness and the meaning I attach to ministering to the ill. This reflection is important for my own clarity and it is important for the effectiveness of my relationships with the patients.

SOCIAL ANAYSIS

From the time I was very little, I was taught the thing to be feared most in life was illness. And not only was illness the most fearful thing there was, it was also the most shameful state I could let myself be in. To be sick was to demonstrate my lack of spiritual competency because I had been taught breathing exercises, meditations, and chants which - if practiced and lived faithfully and competently - were supposed to protect me from all illness. I was told I was God in human form and it was my duty to control the God force in me to keep myself perfectly well. To become ill meant I had shirked my duty.

These values and meanings related to illness have not served me well. They have fostered in me undue anxiety about illness, a strong sense of guilt when I have been sick, and an inappropriate aversion to hospitals. Interestingly, they have not caused me to "look down on" other people who are ill, although I think that message was implicit - if not explicit - in the teachings I was given as a child.

So the meaning of illness for me was evidence of incompetence. Appropriate responses to it were fear, shame, and guilt because I hadn't controlled my life better. Needless to say, my childhood theology of illness needs major reengineering, for my personal benefit as well as for the benefit of those to whom I will minister during their illnesses.

THEOLOGICAL REFLECTION

What meaning do I attach to illness?

I recently read a book by Robert and Jane Alter titled *The Transformative Power of Crisis*. In this book, the Alters say, "Crisis is a turning point in the way one experiences life, a point of transformation." Surely becoming ill and being put in a hospital qualifies as a turning point in the way one experiences life. Visiting patient after patient, I have seen that becoming ill and going to a hospital usually means major things about the patient's life are going to change – sometimes temporarily and sometimes permanently. Adjusting to such changes is central to the crisis of being put in a hospital.

The Alters go on to say, "...the power to use crisis or anything in our lives for transformation is at the core of what it means to be human." This is an important point. It suggests transformation and evolution are the business of being human. It resonates with the Christian beliefs of death and resurrection, of being born again, of being made new.

And then the Alters put the concept of the transforming quality of human crisis into a larger context. They say life is a school, and "All the universe is a university in which all our souls must take all the courses in the curriculum. The name of the curriculum is love." And "when we at last learn to love everything there is – our neighbor as ourself, our earth, life, and God – we've completed the curriculum." Therefore, the crisis of being in the hospital would seem to afford the patient with life coursework if s/he is willing to recognize it and do the coursework. The courses are different for different people, but the Alters believe crises - such as being in the hospital - are filled with opportunity for inner coursework, for inner growth.

The Alters also subscribe to the idea there are no coincidences. That is, everyone you meet and every situation you are in occurs to help you grow. I take a bit of an exception to that thinking. I am not sure everything is divinely directed before it happens, but I do believe that once I make a choice, or someone else makes a choice, or specific circumstances occur, then I am given whatever resources I need to sufficiently handle the situation. But I must listen to the still small voice within me to discern what I may do and what I may learn.

In summary, I ascribe to illness the meaning of an opportunity to grow in some transformative way in the school of life. And I believe the resources to accomplish a meaningful learning or transformation are at hand. Also, I believe the resources – in most instances – are at hand in the patient's inner being, in his/her soul and deepest wisdom.

What meaning do I attach to ministering to the ill?

Ministering to the ill is an enormous privilege and an enormous responsibility because the chaplain can come to the patient at his/her time of crisis and become the facilitator for a healing transformation. As chaplains we can facilitate a conversation between the patient's consciousness and his/her inner wisdom. We can help the patient unpack the layers of deception (denial, ignorance, and limiting beliefs) which are blocking his/her access to learning. We can listen reflectively; help normalize the patient's fears; draw out his/her feelings; offer comfort, gentleness, concern, and prayers. And through all of these behaviors, we can love the patient – helping to dispel his/her fears, shame, guilt and pain – by invoking God's healing, loving presence.

What greater vocation is there than to be called to facilitate healing and gently lead people to God?!

PASTORAL PLANNING

As a result of this reflection, I plan to regard the illnesses of patients non-judgmentally. I will visit patients, believing there are valuable life lessons which can emerge during a visit. I will use facilitation techniques to enable a deep connection between a patient and his/ her inner wisdom and I will remain vigilant in listening to my own inner wisdom during a visit.

I will prayerfully invite God's presence before each visit and I will pray with a patient as s/he is willing at the end of each visit. I will do my best to provide comfort, compassion, understanding, and love during each visit, and I will believe in the possibility of healing transformation occurring in each visit.

May 16, 2000

Today was the last day of this CPE unit. It worked out well. I am both pleased and grateful. Hurray!

The unit I just finished was a part-time unit - we interns were not at the hospital every day. In two weeks I will start a full-time unit for the summer. I will be at the same hospital and have the same supervisor but the floors I work on will be different. I am looking forward to the next unit and I hope things continue to go well.

My Student's Self Evaluation – which I just finished writing – follows.

CLINICAL PASTORAL EDUCATION (CPE)
STUDENT'S SELF EVALUATION
FEBRUARY 2000 – MAY 2000
SUSAN

---

1. Introductory Statement

I undertook this CPE unit to complete an unfinished CPE unit which I started in September 1998 at another location. In late February 1999, I withdrew from that program in order to work with a phobia specialist on past unresolved issues which were negatively impacting my chaplain work. After working with the phobia specialist for nine months, I felt ready to complete my first CPE unit and therefore contacted my former CPE supervisor. Because his current program was full, he referred me to this CPE program.

2. My Clinical Setting

My visitation assignment has been in the Transitional Care Unit. For the most part, this unit supports people who are preparing to leave the hospital and return to private residences, public housing, or other health care facilities. The unit is attended to by doctors, nurses, physical therapists, occupational therapists, and social workers. Often the patients' concerns center around how they will return to their former environments with new restrictions on their lives (e.g. amputations). Pastoral care related to loss is important in this unit.

The Transitional Care Unit has been a good assignment for me to complete my first unit of CPE. It has offered me an environment for ministry where the primary concerns of the patients are usually not death or incapacitating pain. This has allowed me to work on raising my comfort level for simply being in the hospital and visiting people who are ill. In my next CPE unit (this summer), I want to gradually expand my ministry to patients in varying levels of care and types of illnesses.

3. My Learning Goals Set At The Beginning Of This Unit Of CPE With An Evaluation of Fulfillment

Overall Learning Goal: To become a chaplain

A. Personal Objective: To become more comfortable in the hospital setting

I am very pleased and I am very grateful I have made significant progress in my personal objective. Befriending my fears of the hospital setting - and illness in general - has required major personal work for me in order to address my childhood traumas and limiting beliefs. Through the support of a private phobia specialist, the compassionate and skilled support of my CPE supervisor, and personal consciousness-raising and intervention techniques based on the theories of cognitive therapy, I have healed significantly. I look forward to continued growth in this critical area of my development as I enter into a second unit of CPE (a full-time summer unit) next month.

B. Professional Objective: To become a competent pastoral caregiver in the hospital setting

In this CPE unit I have been able to practice many of the pastoral care techniques which I learned in seminary. Additionally, I have learned valuable new techniques from my supervisor in supervisory sessions and from my intern colleagues in interpersonal group sessions. The written assignments for this unit (verbatims, a theological reflection, and a critical incident report) have facilitated significant personal growth for me and have enabled me to become more comfortable in the hospital setting. My associations with hospital staff (nurses, a social worker, an occupational therapist, and a secretary) have taught me the richness of working in a team to provide integrated patient care.

C. Theological Objective: To be a spiritual light and bring people to God

This theological objective is still valid for me. However, I want to enhance my stated means for achieving it based on this CPE experience. In addition to "practicing loving intention and attunement to my inner wisdom of loving guidance," I want to append two other important components. The first is to approach each patient with the understanding that illness is a crisis for the patient and inherent in that crisis is an opportunity for transformational healing. My role then becomes that of a facilitator for transformational healing. The second component is to understand that facilitating transformational healing usually requires evoking the inner wisdom in the patient, in addition to the inner wisdom which resides in me.

4. My Relationship To My Supervisor:

My relationship with my supervisor is a blessed relationship. It has enabled me to experience significant psycho-spiritual growth. For this growth, I am VERY grateful. When I am with my supervisor, I am able to be open, honest, and forthcoming with my fears and concerns. In response, my supervisor is supportive and encouraging. He is highly skilled at listening, analyzing, and providing meaningful feedback.

5. My Relationship To My Peers:

I have enjoyed my intern colleagues very much. We have been able to share deeply and candidly with each other. Each one has enriched my CPE experience.

The Catholic priest in the group risked sharing his deep personal feelings and his humanness in addition to his persona as a priest. I was touched by the courage it took for him to do this and I affirmed his decision to be so open. He indicated to me my deep sharing in the group facilitated his deep sharing.

The Catholic nun in the group brought volumes of religious wisdom to the group. While she chattered on at a somewhat superficial level initially, her pearls of wisdom began to surface in her written work and also in her discourse as the supervisor affirmed her unique gifts and challenged her to recognize and claim her true feelings. With the group's added encouragement, she began to discover where she had learned to suppress her feelings and why she needed to stop doing that. It was a joy to watch her personal identity become more whole.

The Catholic woman in the group brought her passion to minister along with the pain of an impending divorce. Her hospitable nature affirmed each group member and her yearning for learning inspired her valuable questions for the group. I enjoyed her buoyant spirit and I am glad she will be in the summer CPE unit with me.

The Episcopal man brought his youth and his zeal for Christianity. He also brought his over-committed life which was made manifest in his consistently arriving late, in his sometimes falling asleep in the group sessions, and in his leaving immediately at the end of each session (which made it difficult to get to know him as well as the others). I was angry with his behavior and chose to tell him I did not feel I knew him as well as the others because he was so often not around when the rest of us chatted together. He said he was surprised to hear my comments but he made no real effort to change his behavior. The supervisor was compassionate but firm with him, letting him know the patterns he was displaying could alienate parishioners in the future if he let them persist.

6. My Relationship To The Patients To Whom I Ministered:

I have felt comfortable in the role of chaplain with my patients. A number of circumstances contribute to this comfort: the strong sense I have of God's presence in my life, my belief God's presence is inherent in every person's life, my desire to serve, the learnings I have gained from my work in seminary, the skills I bring from a 15 year career as a professional facilitator, and my life experiences as a 55 year old woman.

My relationship to the patients is strongly influenced by my sense that I am extremely privileged to minister to people from the role of chaplain. Therefore, I try to be worthy of this privilege by relating to my patients in a trustworthy, caring, intentional way. I strive to honor each patient's personhood, to respect each patient's inherent worth and dignity at all times, and to gently lead each patient toward God.

7. My Functioning As A Member Of A Team On The Unit:

I have enjoyed working with the nurses, a social worker, an occupational therapist, and a secretary in the Transitional Care Unit. I have felt accepted as a team member and as a valuable resource on the floor. Several times the social worker has asked me to visit a particular patient. I have likewise drawn his attention to a very needy patient. I also had a very rewarding experience coordinating my work with an occupational therapist. These experiences demonstrate to me how effective integrated caretaking can be.

While it did not work out for me to attend "rounds" or other team meetings due to time constraints, I look forward to participating in such meetings in my next CPE unit this summer. I did take responsibility for the chaplain beeper for a week.

8. My Ability To Deal With Stress Situations:

Historically, I have dealt with stressful situations by remaining externally calm and dealing effectively with the issues at hand; then much later I may have been overwhelmed with the feelings which I repressed during the crisis. More recently, and particularly in this CPE unit, I have learned to:

- Recognize the feelings I am having in a stressful situation.
- Experience the feelings for what they are while intentionally drawing on whatever resources I have to deal with them (e.g. yogic breathing, cognitive therapy techniques, asking for assistance).

- Befriend my feelings associated with stress and proceed on through the stressful situation (if it is inappropriate to avoid it).
- Intentionally implement whatever self-care techniques will help me unload the stress when the stressful situation is over (talking to someone, going for a walk, praying, writing in my diary, doing yoga).

9. My Theological Orientation And Ability To Deal With Theological Issues And Integration Into My Role:

I am a Unitarian Universalist. As a young adult I was a United Methodist, and as a child I attended an Episcopal Church while also being taught some Buddhist-like techniques. These facts translate into my being very tolerant and very appreciative of different religious traditions as well as my being more spiritually oriented than religiously oriented. I do consider myself to be theocentric – in my case believing in a compassionate God who is a loving and wise divine presence as well as a sacred, creative, and sustaining energy.

Needless to say, I am very comfortable being with patients of diverse faith traditions as well as patients who are "unchurched," agnostic, or atheistic. I have no interest in evangelizing with patients. I have a lot of interest in facilitating wholistic and spiritual consciousness-raising with patients as they are ready.

10. My Awareness Of Social Conditions, Structures And Systems As Influences On My Ministry:

Courses I have completed in seminary have informed me about the influences which social conditions, structures, and systems may have on my ministry (ethics, family systems, nonviolence, and bereavement). In my personal life, I am currently a member of the Parish Committee in my church. This committee is the governing body of the church, dealing regularly with the social conditions, structures, and systems of the congregation, denomination, town, and world (i.e. outreach). During my career in the business world, I have dealt with dozens and dozens of corporate structures, systems, and social conditions. The seminary courses, my personal experiences, and my work experiences have informed me about the impact social conditions, structures, and systems can have on my ministry.

11. Problem Areas:

My biggest challenges in hospital chaplaincy are (1) being comfortable in the hospital setting, and (2) being comfortable with people who are physically ill. During this CPE Unit I have made major progress in understanding the childhood traumas which have caused my exaggerated fear responses to the hospital setting. I have also made major progress in understanding the psychologically debilitating beliefs which I was given as a child regarding illness. This progress is enabling me to be more and more comfortable with ministering to patients in the hospital and I now look forward to continuing my progress in the next CPE unit this summer.

12. Progress Made:

As stated in #11 above, I have made significant progress in becoming comfortable and competent to minister in the hospital setting and I am looking forward to my next CPE unit, a full-time unit scheduled for this summer. In the summer unit, I hope to deepen my ministerial skills in pastoral care and expand my comfort for ministering in many different types of hospital units (intensive care, hospice, emergency room, etc.).

June 7, 2000

The new CPE full-time unit started last week. My visitations are on both the Transitional Care floor (where I did visitations during the previous

CPE unit) and also the Oncology floor. The Oncology floor is located far away from the chaplain's office – across a street and down a block on the other side of this very large hospital complex.

Today I turned in my first verbatim. It describes one of my visits on the Oncology floor. I will never forget this visit or the patient involved. Our time together seemed to have a transcendent quality to it. The verbatim follows.

CPE
VERBATIM
JUNE 7, 2000

Chaplain: Susan
Date of Visit: June 13, 2000
Date of Admission: May 31, 2000   **Unit:** Oncology
Age: 55   **Sex:** F   **Marital Status:** M   **No. of Children:** 1
Religious Preference: RCA **Congregation/Parish:** Unknown
Admitting Diagnosis: Lung/brain cancer
Length of Visit: 15 minutes

SUMMARY:

The day before this visit, I met the patient and her family. The patient's sister was standing outside the room as I walked by and looked in. I saw what seemed to be a party going on with balloons and a bride and groom statue on a table. I greeted the sister who told me the patient was dying of lung cancer which had metastasized to the brain. The patient and the patient's husband had renewed their wedding vows the day before and that was the reason for the decorations. The patient was the oldest of seven sisters. This sister, and the patient, and their mother had all smoked. Their mother died of lung cancer the previous December. Now this sister was trying to stop smoking.

The sister mentioned she had been thinking about calling a chaplain to come to see the patient. All of the siblings had been raised Roman Catholic, but the patient had given up the religion thirty years before. When she recently got sick, the patient came back to the religion.

The sister asked me if I would come back later when the rest of the family would arrive, in order that everyone could stand around the patient's bed and say a prayer together. I said I would come back. Then I asked her if she wanted me to meet the patient right then and also come back later. She said "yes" and took me into the room where I briefly met the patient and two other sisters.

I was introduced as the Chaplain to the patient and her sisters. Then I was asked if we could all say the "Our Father" together. All of us prayed the "Our Father" together, and shortly thereafter, I left.

I returned about five o'clock and met the patient's husband, her son, a few other family members and many friends who came into the room one after the other in a steady stream. I was once again introduced as the chaplain and asked to say the "Our Father" with everyone standing around the bed holding hands. We did what was asked and then the family began to show me the wedding pictures of the patient and her husband. The couple had been married for 32 years. The pictures showed an extremely beautiful bride and a very handsome groom. There was a lot of hubbub in the room as the relatives and friends visited and came and went. I wondered how this very sick patient could endure so much noise and confusion. During this visit and the previous one I longed to have some quiet time with the patient.

When I left the room I walked out with another visitor who works at the hospital. She used to work with the patient who was a nurse at the hospital for twenty-two years. I learned the patient had established a program to encourage high school students to go into nursing. She was obviously a very wonderful human being. During the limited time I visited with her in the first two meetings I sensed the spirit of a lovely, beautiful soul.

PLANS:

I decided to return to the patient's room the next morning about 11:00 am. While I did not know who would be in the room with the patient, I was hoping for some quiet time with her in order that I might pray with her in an extemporaneous way. I wanted to pray for God's love to envelop her and for her to be granted peace of mind and heart as she experienced the mystery of life, including its earthly end. I wanted her to have more to draw on spiritually than just the perfunctory reciting of the "Our Father" which seemed to be the family's key touch stone for their religion. And yet with this hope in my heart, I was prepared to simply be present with the patient and family in a way which would be acceptable and comfortable for them.

OBSERVATIONS:

I looked into the patient's room from the hall. The patient's husband was sitting in a chair by the side of the patient's bed. He was a handsome man with thinning dark hair, dark eyes, and a moderate build. He wore a long sleeved shirt, dress slacks and dress shoes. The patient was asleep and he appeared to be simply studying her every feature. He looked up as I stood in the doorway and called to me, "Susan."

As I went into the room to greet him and the patient, I heard a small radio softly playing classical music. The radio was on the table in front of the window along with the balloons, the bride and groom statues, and the wedding photo book I had looked at the day before.

The patient was propped up in the only bed in the room. Her head was bald and her mouth hung open as she slept. Her face was still pretty in spite of her horrible illness. Her skin looked smooth and she had a soft feminine appearance. She did not appear gaunt or too thin and her fingernails were nicely manicured with a whitish nail polish. She wore her engagement and wedding rings. She was probably 115 pounds and 5'4" tall. She had large soft lips and her cheeks and neck seemed roundish and puffy. She had IV needles in her lower right arm, and a stand holding the IV bottles was on her right side. The sheet came up to her waist.

THE VISIT: (H=Husband, C=Chaplain, P=Patient)

C1 Hello H. How are things going today?

H1 She is more congested today. (He stood to wake P and tell her I was there.)

C2 No need to wake her. Let her rest. She had a lot of visitors last night.

H2 Yes, that was important to her.

C3 I'm sure it was…May I pull up this stool and visit with you for a while?

H3 Yes.

C4 (I pulled the stool over near his chair.) When I was leaving yesterday, I walked out with a woman who was here visiting and who had worked with P.

H4 Was it XX?

C5 No…It was N.M.

H5 Oh, yes. They worked together for many years.

C6 She told me P was involved in teaching and setting up a program to encourage young people to become nurses.

H6 Yes. She set up a program called "Choose Nursing." It was for inner city blacks. She worked very hard to get a 1.5 million dollar grant for it. It offered sophomore girls in high school the chance to learn about nursing. And it also provided the tutoring help they needed to prepare them to go to nursing school.

H7 (Then P moved her leg and opened her eyes. H got up and bending over P said to her) P, Susan - the Chaplain – is here.

C7 (I walked around to the other side of the bed and P reached out to hold my hand.) Hello, P. It is nice to see you again.

P1 Thank you. (Her words were said at a barely audible volume.)

H7 Hold up your badge so she can see where you are from.

C8 (I held up my badge.) I am from the Chaplain's Office.

H8 She is looking at your pin.

C9 (I held my lapel pin so that she could see it better.) It is an angel with a heart. (P studied the pin and I waited quietly.)

H9 (Turning to P) Do you want to say the "Our Father" with Susan? (P nodded yes. With H and me holding Ps hands, the three of us said the "Our Father." I kept my eyes open to see what P was doing. She said the words very softly with us while keeping her eyes open. When the prayer was over she took her hand away. I decided to try to visit with her just a little.

C10 H was telling me about the program you put together to encourage young people to become nurses. What a wonderful thing to do.

P2 (Barely audibly she spoke) Choose nursing.

C11 Yes, you called it "Choose Nursing." You helped many young people with that program. (P tried to say more but neither H nor I could understand what she was saying, although I put my head down very near to her lips to try to understand her words.)

C12 It's okay. You just rest now.

H10 Yes, just rest now.

C13 (I looked at P for a moment and then knew I wanted to try to pray extemporaneously with her.) P, would it be OK if I said an extemporaneous prayer with you before I leave? (P nodded "yes" and reached out to take my hand.)

C14 (I took her hand, shut my eyes, and began to pray.) Eternal and loving God, be present with us now and envelop P and H in your perfect love. Grant them your peace to heal their minds and their hearts as they experience the mystery of life. Receive also their gratitude for the support of their family and friends, and for the doctors and nurses, and others who are caring for P. In Jesus' name we pray. Amen

H11 Thank you.

C15 (I nodded at H and then smiled at P. She tried to say something, and I leaned over and put my ear up close to her face to try to understand her words.)

P3 (She seemed to ask...) Are you from the other side?

C16 (I thought she meant the other side of the hospital complex where the Chaplain's Office is. Therefore, I smiled and said...) Yes.

(Then P looked up at me and raised her chin.)

H11 She wants to kiss you.

C17 (Realizing H was right, I hesitated for a moment...and then gently kissed P on her lips, and she kissed me back.)

H12 Thank you.

C18 God bless. (I smiled and nodded at H and P, and then left the room.)

PASTORAL OPPORTUNITY:

The circumstances of this visit offered a number of opportunities for providing pastoral care.

Spending a little time "alone" with P's husband was the first opportunity. I was able to give him time to remember and share P's work and to honor her by so doing. Had P not awakened when she did, I might have been able to learn more about H and how P's dying was effecting him.

There was also the opportunity to provide a comforting religious ritual for P and H, by saying the "Our Father" with them. This ritual seemed to be the family's primary way to "be religious" together.

Offering the extemporaneous prayer was my way of introducing P and H to a different way of doing spiritual connection. I think the prayer may have served that purpose as it seemed to prompt P's desire to ask me if I were from "the other side." I now suspect that P's question was not about the other side of the hospital complex, but rather the other side of human life. And after she asked that question - to which I answered "yes" - she looked at me and raised her chin, wanting to kiss me. I wonder if the kiss was a way for P to express her desire to embrace a spiritual connection between herself and God, before she left this planet.

July 13, 2000

Today at CPE I turned in a verbatim for a visit I made two days ago on the Transitional Care floor. What a privilege it was for me to experience this visit! The verbatim follows.

CPE
VERBATIM

Chaplain: Susan   **Date:** 7/11/2000

Date of Admission: 6/19/2000   **Unit:** TCU

Age: 82   **Sex:** F   **Marital Status:** W   **No. of Children:** None

Religious Preference: RCA **Congregation/Parish:** Unknown

Admitting Diagnosis: Hip Fracture

Additional Information:

Case Management Meeting

In the case management meeting, I learned A had been doing well but had recently become depressed. It was noted she was very sad about the death of a nephew not too long ago.

A Nurse

A nurse on the floor asked me to see A. She explained A had worked at the hospital in the Human Resources department for years and before that she had worked at another medical center. She said A had been a bright, well-respected and well-liked employee. The nurse was at a loss regarding how to help A regain her desire to live.

The Patient

A told me her nephew, B, came to live with her and her husband the day after the nephew was born, when his mother died as a result of child birth. A raised B as if he were her own child. After A's husband died, B moved back in with A and took care of her. A said they were the best of friends, taking trips together and enjoying life together. B never married. He died suddenly of a heart attack in February of this year. A said B kissed her good morning every morning and kissed her goodnight every night. She said they really enjoyed each other's company.

Patient's Primary Concern: A was in physical pain from her hip rehabilitation, and she was grieving the death of her nephew.

Visit Number (with this patient): 6

Length of Visit: 20 minutes

SUMMARY:

In the previous five visits I got to know A quite well. She told me a lot about her relationship with her nephew. She cried frequently. I could see the waves of sadness overtake her. She didn't see how she could ever get over this loss and go on living. She also complained a lot about her many physical pains related to her hip fracture. I became aware her physical pain and her moods seemed to go up and down in peaks and valleys. She is a very sensitive woman, both to physical pain and to emotional pain.

A also complained consistently about the climate of the room which was too hot for her and too cold for her roommate. Yet she and her roommate liked each other and talked to each other a lot. Often when I came to visit, I would visit with both women concurrently. Because of this scenario I did not offer to pray with the women for the first few visits. Then one day when they both seemed particularly "down," I asked A if she would like me to say a prayer. She said "yes." She seemed to greatly appreciate the prayer. The other woman seemed to like it too.

After one visit in which A was particularly fearful, I decided to loan her a favorite book of mine titled *To Heal Again*. It is basically a bereavement book with a painting and a few words per page. It had helped me when I was grieving and I had given it to others who found it helpful during times of their bereavements. A kept the book overnight and thanked me for it, saying it helped her.

PLANS:

My plan for this visit was to observe how A was doing physically and emotionally and then respond to her needs with compassion, using prayer if the situation that day seemed right for it.

OBSERVATIONS:

I entered the room and saw A's roommate sitting in her chair as was usually the case when I came to visit. I greeted her while noting the curtain between her and A was drawn. The curtain had not been drawn in any of my previous visits. I could hear A moaning in pain as I approached the curtain.

I peeked around the curtain and saw A lying in the bed, her face grimaced in pain. She is a tiny, beautiful, older woman with lovely, fluffy, white hair which is cut stylishly in a short cut. She has vivid blue eyes and glasses with clear frames. Her face is very soft looking and relatively unlined for her age. She probably weighs 95 lbs. and is about 4'10" tall. When she does smile, she looks like the grandma anyone would love to have. I liked her immediately the first time I saw her. Today, she looked up at me and called out, "Oh, I need to see you today."

THE VISIT (C=Chaplain, P=Patient):

C1   Hello A.

P1   Oh, I need to see you today. I'm in such pain. I have a skin rash on my back. I can't lie down or sit up.

C2   Oh dear.

P2   I was sick last night. But they got me up this morning and then they let me go back to sleep until 10:30. Nobody looked in on me and the aide is mean.

C3   I am sorry you are so uncomfortable. (Noticing how panicky she seemed, I decided to try having her breathe a simple breathing exercise to help her get rid of the panic.) A, let me give you a little breathing exercise to help you calm down. (She seemed willing.) I want you to inhale while I count to 4. Ready? Inhale 1,2,3,4. Now exhale 1,2,3,4. Now breathe normally. (She wasn't able to follow the directions very well but she was trying.) Let me show you how to do it. First, I will breathe in for four counts, and then I will breathe out for four counts. (I demonstrated for her.) Now you try. Inhale 1,2,3,4. Now exhale 1,2,3,4. (She still wasn't getting it right but she continued to try.) Now this time when you breathe in, imagine you are breathing in lots of healing energy. Then hold your breath for four counts while you imagine healing energy spreading throughout your body. Then when you exhale, let every muscle relax. Okay? (She nodded "yes.") Ready, inhale now, imagining healing energy coming into your body. Now hold your breath and imagine the healing energy spreading out in your body. Now exhale and let your whole body relax. Relax all of your muscles. There, that's better. (She wasn't able to follow the directions very well, but she tried and she had settled down quite a bit during the process.) (Pause) Yesterday when I saw you, you were doing so well.

P3　Yes, I was.

C4　You know you go up and down. (I moved my hand to trace an up and down cycle.) Although you may feel you are in a valley today, you were better yesterday and you will be better again. (She seemed to brighten at that comment.)

P4　I'm so hot. My roommate is freezing and I am unbearably hot.

C5　Yes, it is hot on this side of the room and it is cold on your roommate's side. There is another room down the hall which has the same problem. Unfortunately, it's the way the rooms are designed.

P5　There was a conference last night and they are going to move me to the S.M. hospital. Do you go there?

C6　No. Is that a rehabilitation hospital?

P6　Yes. Hopefully, I will be more comfortable there.

C7　So, you are looking forward to that move?

P7　Oh yes. Can we do that exercise again? I want to be sure I know how to do it.

C8 Yes. There are three parts to it. First, you inhale for four counts. Then you hold your breath for four counts. Then you exhale for four counts. (We tried it a few more times. Then I told her to just breathe normally. After a few moments I continued.) A, would you like me to say a prayer today?

P8 Yes, let's do that.

C9 Eternal, loving, and compassionate God, be present with us now. Envelop A in your healing love and enable her to feel your peace. Help her to know that whenever she is feeling anxious, she can connect with your peace; and in that peace she can have faith you are always with her. Help her to know that even in her pain, you are providing her with what she needs. (All of a sudden, A started to sob and called out…)

P9 Oh, I can feel my nephew is here. He is praying for me. (I opened my eyes, and seeing and feeling the intensity which she was experiencing, I took her hand. She went on with great clarity.) You know, I didn't help him when he died. I couldn't have saved him, but I didn't try.

C10 (Gently and softly I responded to what she had just said.) So you feel some guilt about that?

P10 Yes. I'm releasing that feeling right now. My nephew is happy. He wants me to be happy too. (More tears)

C11 Good, A. The guilt is not necessary.

P11 For the first time, it has left me.

C12 Oh A, I'm so glad.

P12 (Suddenly) I have to go to the bathroom. (Startled, I said "okay" and inquired whether I should get a nurse to help her. She said "no" and pulled herself up to sit on the edge of the bed. Then she took hold of her walker, pulled herself to a standing position and made her way to the bathroom. I waited until she came out of the bathroom and put herself back in bed. Settled once again, she looked up at me and said…) I didn't know how much I needed you today. Thank you for coming.

C13 (Smiling) You're welcome. I'll see you tomorrow.

P13 Thank you for coming.

C14 (Nodding) Bye bye.

PASTORAL OPPORTUNITY:

The patient needed validation of her misery, both physically and emotionally. She also needed to be calmed from the panic she was experiencing. With these needs addressed, she became open to a moment of spiritual healing which she later called "my breakthrough." Prayer was, I believe, the catalyst for her breakthrough. It ushered in the grace which she so very much needed and was given, a sense of her nephew's presence with her, the understanding that her nephew is happy now, and the information that her nephew wants her to be happy too. This grace also let the patient identify and release the guilt she had been holding over not trying to do something to help her nephew when he had his heart attack.

ANALYSIS: THE PATIENT

Theological Concerns:

The patient is Roman Catholic. Her faith is important to her and has been helpful to her. On the other hand, I suspect she has not been taught to pray extemporaneously by, and for, herself. I think it might help her enormously if she could begin to do this. With her high degree of sensitivity - her emotions and thoughts are very close to the surface - she could learn to lift them up to God in extemporaneous prayer and probably find great solace and divine wisdom in doing so.

Psychological Concerns:

The patient's highly sensitive psychological nature is both a blessing and a curse for her. As expressed in "THE VISIT" above, she tends to go through peaks and valleys emotionally. I hope by understanding this pattern of behavior she can begin to manage the peaks and valleys better, intentionally trying to believe there will be a better tomorrow when she is down, and conversely understanding sadness will occur again even though she is experiencing an "up" period.

Obviously, the patient has been going through a difficult bereavement process. While I know she will have low moments for quite some time to come, my sense is that this hospital stay provided some time for her to do intense grieving which she needed to do in order to get on the other side of the depression and dysfunctionality she has been experiencing.

Sociological Concerns:

The patient lives in a condo where she has friends. She also has a step-niece whom she says is wonderful to her and who will help her when she leaves the hospital. The patient enjoyed her roommate in the hospital and also seemed to enjoy interacting with the nurses, OTs, PTs, and social worker - when she was not experiencing a lot of physical pain. In my last visit with her, when she was feeling much better physically and emotionally, she was quite delightful socially. She spoke of books, her job, and her other interests - as well as showing a lot of interest and encouragement for me in my ministry.

THE CHAPLAIN:

As I wrote above, I immediately liked the patient when I met her. Ministering to her during many visits gave me the opportunity to really get to know her and to provide the best care for her I knew how to give. It was very gratifying for me to have her respond to the many pastoral care techniques I have been taught. It was particularly meaningful for me to be with her when she felt her nephew's presence and seemed to connect with him in a deeply spiritual and healing way. I think it was a privilege for both of us to share the time we had together. I experienced it as sacred time, I think she did too.

August 9, 2000

Today was the last day of this CPE unit. I did it and I'm thrilled! I am also very grateful for many things. First, at the risk of seeming self-centered, I am extraordinarily grateful I was able to finish this unit without being encumbered by paralyzing trauma imprints from my past. Whoopee! I was able to be comfortable in the hospital setting and I learned I am a capable chaplain intern. I am also deeply grateful for my supervisor's support and wisdom, my intern colleagues' sharing and caring, and the privilege to meet so many wonderful patients and hospital personnel. Hallelujah and Amen!

October 25, 2000

I can't believe I am thinking about this. As much as I <u>love</u> where I live, I have started thinking about moving back to where I grew up. I am shocked that I am considering this. What has caused me to think about it?

I guess I am lonesome to live near "family." My beloved stepmother and her sister, as well as my nephew and his young family, live where I grew up. My best friend from high school still lives there too and my dear college roommate lives a two-hour drive away. These people are all very important to me. Having finished two chaplain internships and the seminary courses I wanted to take, perhaps it is time for me to go back "home" and build a new life there.

Betty (my wonderful stepmother) and Alice (my wonderful step aunt) have been the two most important women in my life. For me as a young adult they modeled how to live a life of love, joy, connection, caring, and giving

- while being grounded in Christian teachings. Now, to my utter dismay, both of them have been diagnosed with Alzheimer's disease. I want to be there to support them during their difficult times now and in the future.

This move is a lot to think about. I have loved living here soooooooo much. I will miss the beauty of nature which surrounds me. Every day I have been blessed by this beauty. Where I grew up simply does not have such natural beauty. Leaving this particular location will create a deep sense of loss for me.

Oh my, there is so much to think about and put into place if I am going to move back "home"…

October 28, 2000
I have become happy and excited about moving back to where I grew up! I just called Pat, my best friend in high school. I called her to set up a time for us to get together when I fly back home in early November for Betty's birthday. During my conversation with Pat, she mentioned the names of our high school classmates who recently got together to start planning for our 40th high school reunion. (Has it really been 40 years? Yikes!) The reunion will be held next June. Perhaps I can work things out to move back before the reunion.

I told Pat I am thinking about moving back. She was thrilled to hear this news. Tomorrow I will call Carolyn, my favorite college roommate, to set up a time to see her too.

November 6, 2000
I'm at the airport after having a wonderful time visiting my relatives and friends. I stayed one night with Pat and spent one afternoon with Carolyn. What a treat to spend time with both of my long-time friends!

The rest of the time I stayed at my nephew's home. Ron, Annie, and their two-year-old daughter, Alison, made the visit very special for me. They all seemed delighted to have me there and to learn I may be moving back. Alison is beautiful in every way - full of love, and spirit, and joy. When I move back, spending time with her will provide me with experiences of nurturing and loving a new little soul on this earth.

Seeing Betty and Alice laughing and enjoying being with family members was an enormous thrill for me. The birthday celebration was lots of fun. Their spirits are still joyful and loving despite the great travail they are both experiencing with Alzheimer's disease. I love them so much! I hope I will be able to make a truly positive difference in their lives when I move back.

There was one incident which provided a reason for Annie not to embrace me fully. She spoke of the "sin" of homosexually that is infusing itself into the organizations of Boy Scouts and Girl Scouts. I responded that I do not think homosexuality is a sin. In the discussion which followed I also acknowledged I do not believe I will go to hell because I do not accept Jesus as my savior. I suspect Annie may be strongly conflicted between accepting me, and not accepting me because I believe differently from her and Ron. I surely hope they don't abandon me in the future; but I do think that is a possibility, given their conservative religious belief system and their likely fear of my being a satanic influence on their daughter. Sigh...

November 8, 2000

I am continuing to be excited about moving back to where I grew up. I love the thought of living near Ron, Annie, and Alison...a family for me. And on the other end of the life spectrum, it feels good and right to be near Betty and Alice to help with their ongoing care.

And then there's my third chaplain internship which I just started researching. Once I have moved, I want to continue my work to become an accredited chaplain, and then I will be able to be a "light worker" into my old age. Becoming a chaplain seems like the right role for me…although I do still fear whether or not I really can be okay long-term in the medical environment. Time will tell about that…

December 12, 2000
Dear God,
Wow! Wow! Wow! I am at the airport after two of the most nourishing weeks of my life. THANK YOU, GOD, FOR YOUR PRESENCE through my family, my friends, the condo shopping experience, and the chaplain internship interview. How great Thou art!

In six months, I will be with my wonderful family in a gorgeous new condo near them; my high school and college friends will be close by; a UU church will be ten minutes down the road; and I will have the opportunity to work in the hospital internship program which just accepted me for my third unit of CPE. I feel whole, complete, satisfied, grateful, and abundantly blessed by Your grace.

Thank you for Your love, God.
Susan

January 24, 2001
This is a strange time for me. I have chosen to make this month my time to prepare for the next phase of my life, by weeding out "things" I don't want or need to take with me when I move. I am blessed to have this time and yet it is strange to now be disciplining myself to clean out closets, drawers, files, etc.

Today I cleaned out the "treasures drawer" in my bedroom. I threw many things out, yet I kept family cards and other particularly meaningful notes. When I cleaned out the filing cabinets, I decided to keep the files with materials from each of the five men I dated during the past ten years since I left Dean. I am realizing each of these men – and Dean – had attributes and behaviors which informed me about myself and life in general.

— Dean, like my mother, was highly narcissistic. He also had admirable traits like being ambitious and courageous. Neither he nor my mother hesitated to try new things and make them work out. I think I am ambitious and courageous too and I am glad I learned these attributes from my mother and Dean. They keep me going, enrich my life, and help me survive and thrive.

— Michael, before I met him, was sensitive yet closed emotionally. When we met, we both opened up immediately. Together we experienced a rich, deep, authentic, caring and sharing love…until, alas, he was pulled back into his family's ethic of prioritizing the needs of his wife and the family's cultural values over his own needs and desires. So in my relationship with Michael, I was challenged again (as with Dean at the end of our relationship) to set healthy boundaries for myself regarding a significant other, and to do so by caring and loving myself <u>first</u>. Unfortunately, I continued for a <u>very</u> long time to project onto Michael the self-care values I had recently learned for myself. In reality, he could not hold the same values for self-care as I. And it was very unfortunate I had not yet learned to detach <u>in a timely way</u> from the emotional abandonment experience with Michael. I suspect my long-time survival technique - of projecting onto others the traits I wanted them to have - kept me attached emotionally to Michael much longer than was healthy or appropriate…unless, of course, traumas from previous emotional abandonment(s) had not yet been thoroughly processed – duh!

— I dated a man named Shawn. He was authentic, stable, and well-established professionally. He told me he didn't know what love was, although he said we could talk about marriage if I wanted to. Strangely, I enjoyed our sexual relationship a lot, even though I was not romantically attracted to him. I did appreciate his authenticity, stability, and professionalism. I want those attributes to be my attributes too.

— Bret was young, very spiritual, interested in nature and outdoor activities, and very disdainful about the material world. When we rode in his car the road was visible through the floor boards, and riding in his car during the summer months was excruciatingly hot. That scenario didn't work for me. I enjoy basic creature comforts. I remember Bret told me once that being in my home was like being in a magazine. Sigh…For me, being in an attractive and orderly home is important. Such an environment was uncomfortable for Bret. Yet he was a lovely man in many ways, and I greatly value his spiritual sensitivities and the fun times we shared. I sincerely hope he finds someone who is just right for him and they are very happy together.

— Peter was charming, affectionate, and decent. He was an older man and a family man with children and grandchildren. It turned out he was also commitment avoidant. I suspect this circumstance resulted from his insufficient grieving for his wife who had died four years earlier. I enjoyed Peter but I needed him to want marriage as I did. He couldn't go there.

— Randy was attractive to me looks-wise, career-wise, and age-wise. Over time, however, I perceived in him a severe lack of positive self-esteem. This lack seemed to manifest with me in his use of mind games which I experienced as psychologically and emotionally abusive. While I wish Randy well, I am glad I chose - in a reasonable amount of time - to end our relationship.

I think I may be in a process of integrating the many pieces of my life. I seem to have reached a point where I don't need to fight, fear, or deny my previous relationships with others, nor my previous life experiences which seemed life-depleting for me. Rather, I am gratefully acknowledging all of my relationships and life experiences as part of who I am. And I honor these relationships and experiences, feeling blessed by their presence in my life. I believe all of them have helped me become who I was designed to be.

May 11, 2001

I've cried a lot today – tears of great joy after I received a Mother's Day card from Ron, Annie, and Alison. It is a lovely card and Annie wrote, "We are so thankful you are part of our family and soon to be our neighbor!"

What wonderful words to receive. Words from my family members who really do want me to be close by and a part of their lives. I am feeling very blessed!

May 17, 2001

It is 4:30 a.m. Can't sleep. I really am moving and I feel the hope and the excitement and the smallest bit of "Oh my God, this is a big step…a big change…a big effort." All of that is in my mind, heart, and body…along with trust in myself and my choice to move!

Last night, nine of my teacher friends from twenty-two years ago had a goodbye party for me at my favorite restaurant. It was a wonderful, fun, and very celebrative time. Old friends are so dear and so important to have. I will miss being near these friends and attending get-togethers with them.

May 20, 2001

Five weeks from today the movers arrive! Ron called last night and offered to fly here the day before the movers come and then chauffer me in my car back to "our" hometown. Yippee!!! He is such a thoughtful young man. It will be great fun to spend two days driving with him and I am relieved I don't have to drive alone. The real estate closing on my new place will happen in the late afternoon of the day we arrive. I will stay with Ron and his family until the movers appear a day or two later.

ONWARD!

Made in the USA
Middletown, DE
03 January 2020